# DOWN IS UP

## THE DREAM LINE

### HINDSIGHT, FORESIGHT, INSIGHT

*Anthony M Malcolm Jr*

# DEDICATION

Grab your favorite beverage, we're about to dive into a
good book.

## "DOWN IS UP"

## *The Dream Line*

*I dedicate this book to every dreamer, visionary, and
believer. I pray you find pearls in this book, that you
can apply in efforts to become a better you,*

*May God guide you along your journey.*

*LOVE, A.M*

# Table of Contents

# INTRODUCTION

I woke up to everyone calling me Pastor Malcolm, Apostle, Prophet, or Bishop. Honestly, it was all really scary for me. It sort of made me very uncomfortable and a little worried. If you really want to know me, you should know that I'm an introvert. Not to mention, I struggle with always feeling unworthy and not good enough. Hearing my name next to prestigious titles gave me goosebumps.

Don't get me wrong, I love Jesus Christ, and I revere the things of God. However, me, A pastor? Is this a joke? I'm constantly questioning myself, Am I deserving? I'm so imperfect, Lord, I'm your worst son, I've done so much against you before I really knew you. My life isn't even all together.

I've never aspired to do anything in ministry. I never aspired to a title or a position in the church. So, my question is, when did these titles and authority come into the mind of God's people?

Especially when referring to me or about me. I am aware that there was a shift that took place in my life. I wasn't trained or coached for it. I kept telling myself I wasn't ready. At least to become anything, the people of God were calling me. So, how did this happen?

A lot of people desire to elevate, in life, in ministry, and in the church today. There are a countless number of people who desire titles and positions, notoriety, power, and influence, which all come with the titles. A Lot of individuals desire to operate in multiple levels of spheres in the realms of Christianity.

Personally, I think desiring those things are great, but very few really understand what it takes to achieve such desires. Some people get discouraged along the way. Some have not recognized who they are in the body of Christ. Some are in schools and degree programs, taking various classes for it. A select few were born for it.

What I'm trying to say is some were called to it, and some were chosen for it. There are some people who don't even realize that God is calling them or that God has chosen them. Better yet, some refuse to acknowledge it.

Reading can open the eye of understanding, understanding who you are, maybe even spark the flame of figuring out what God desires for you. This is the Langu of "Down is Up!" The dream line.

I'm a very creative individual, constantly thinking about ways to excite and edify anyone who reads my books. I not only want you to read for knowledge and understanding but also for enjoyment. Who wants to read a boring book? I know I wouldn't, and that's just me being blunt.

To appease that creativity, I filled this book with not only a story, but with invaluable lessons in lessons, deeper meanings uniquely written in The Langu of "SIGHT."

The ability to see is something that can be natural and supernatural. This book will have some spiritual aspects that tell the story of my journey in a way that others can learn from life, which is the Word. The Bible can come alive and does in this book.

The Langu of "Down is Up" is based on the understanding that there are three kinds of "SIGHT." These are ways to look at your life in a different type of light, to push you forward and not keep you stuck or stagnant. Especially for those of you who are walking the dream line. Which is a very trying journey.

Firstly, "HINDSIGHT," These sections will be my story. Telling you about my journey of how I arrived where I am today. Each story corresponds with another sight section.

This brings us to "INSIGHT." This section will dive deeper into understanding the lessons and themes of each chapter. Introspection also speaks to discernment. Being aware of your own mental health is vital and important to having a healthy lifestyle with sound decision making.

This type of sight can be a gift given to different individuals. So that we can understand what's taking place at the moment for many different reasons, not just for the individual but also for others. Insight will help us navigate situations and circumstances with a high level of confidence. Woven into this section will be therapeutic practices that you can take and implement in your day to day. Some of you will be able to take them and make them your own.

Lastly, "FORESIGHT." This will be the section of the book where we get into the word of God. Asking the questions but understanding the answer is "God's will." This section brings the word alive and speaks directly to those walking the dream line.

These sections will be woven together with scriptures to show parallels. It's important to remember that God has a plan for your life. That plan is to prosper you. Having the presence of mind in all situations that, although we cannot definitively say where God is bringing us, we can still understand that God is in complete control.

Taking the nuances of each chapter to show how each moment is like a course taken in the university of "God's Plan," where the curriculum is based on where he wants to bring you. As you read these sections, you will begin to see the handiwork of God in life, and your life will start to make sense.

Take these nuances, lessons, and tools and apply them to where you currently are. Sometimes, God did something for us, and we are unaware of that. My goal is for you, the reader, to not pray for your physical now but your supernatural tomorrow, fully submitting and going into the depths of Christ so that you can go higher in life, ministry, and fulfill the dreams and visions God has placed in you.

Things that might have deeper meanings, or more to the story, or just a really good quotable. I'll leave a *"LANGU,"* this is so you and I can acknowledge the deep moments, take a minute, and really pay attention to those think pieces. - *"LANGU"*

# Hindsight

The "Hindsight" sections are about my origin story, how I got to this point. Sometimes, when you share and are transparent, it can help others understand who you are, and also help them push through the tough times. Often time, we only share the good and try to forget the ugly. This section is meant to share the truth. So we can let go and be free to soar into new heights.

# Chapter 1

# HINDSIGHT - COVID

During The Tail-end of the bizarre Covid-19 pandemic, I found myself in a dark space. In college, I worked in the school system and worked part-time at the hospital. I was struggling mentally and emotionally. I met the mother of my first two children, A year prior to me starting these jobs. Truthfully, I really tried to step up and start to build a life for her, my daughter, and myself. Working about 70 hours every week was draining, but it was for them. At least I wasn't struggling financially, but something still felt off. Everything started out good, but eventually took a turn for the worse. Home life started becoming toxic, and with the nature of my Jobs, I became mentally drained.

It was like the peace and the happiness I started building just crumbled before my eyes. As a result, I started smoking more and more and leaned towards drinking alcohol to take the edge off. I began drinking bottles of alcohol every day.

Although things were rocky at home, I still tried to maintain my mental health. I kept showing up for work, trying to hold things together. Eventually, one day, I cracked. I felt like I was literally drowning. In rooms filled with people, I felt alone. In moments where I should be happy, the thought of how my life was falling apart plagued my emotions.

So, I continued to smoke weed until it numbed me mentally and emotionally. It became a way of escape for me. Unbeknown to me at the time, I'd taken on a whole new personality once I was intoxicated. My drink of choice was hennessy and champagne, or hennessy mixed with wine. My days quickly consisted of me drinking all day from sun up to sun down.

I never wanted to be around anyone for too long because I just wanted to be alone to drink and smoke. However, I've always found solace in music. I've always found solace in creating. Music was something that had been a part of my life on and off for years.

It's interesting how the combination of events in my life pushed me into a place where I shutdown. To be completely honest, I was a functioning alcoholic and pothead. However, the loneliness and stress pushed me into a creative space I'd never been in before.

I began meeting new people and working with various artists and producers. Most of the artists at the time were heavily in the dancehall diaspora. One of them happened to be a cousin of mine. How ironic to find out that he only lived around the corner from my apartment.

Not only did he enjoy smoking and drinking, but he also had a home studio in his basement. In hopes of getting away from my home life, I started spending a lot of my free time there. Sometimes recording music, sometimes playing video games, sometimes just freestyling songs on different riddims until we'd run out of lyrics. Oftentimes discussing life and his journey in the music industry, and the different people he had encountered.

One thing I love doing is learning, I find that everyone you encounter can teach you something if you just listen. I never got a good opportunity to really know my father. The circumstances were beyond our control at the time. However, talking with my cousin made me feel like I was getting to know more about my dad. Something that I felt like I needed at that point in time.

Ultimately, I was learning more about where my creativity came from. Hearing stories about my dad, cousins, aunts, uncles, and his side of the family intrigued me. For the first time, I started to feel validated, wanted, and accepted for who I was, especially with the creativity that I had and the creation of music, art, and fashion.

As it would turn out, I come from a long line of musicians and artists. This pushed me to research, and I found out that I am related to the late great Bob Marley somewhere in my lineage. It's safe to say that music is in my blood, but more importantly influence was a part of my bloodline.

During the pandemic, I traveled to Jamaica for the first time by myself. This trip was a spur of the moment trip. When I landed in Jamaica, I was both nervous and excited. I did not know what to expect, nor did I have any plans.

The whole world was on lock-down, but not the warm, sunny island of Jamaica. I called a very close cousin to pick me up from the Norman-manely Kingston airport. Quickly, we zipped through the city in his silver car, talking about music and getting into the studio. He began to tell me that the voice that I have is very unique, and I should look into fusing my style with some afrobeats.

After driving to the local Cambio, which is a place in the islands where you can exchange money. I had to stock up on my weed and liquor. I asked my cousin where we could get the best weed Jamaica had to offer.

He brought me to what looked like an apartment, he left the car running and ran into a back door. About 5 minutes later, he brought out almost a quarter pound of weed. I remember thinking to myself, "Gosh, this weed smells amazing."

We quickly drove away to the Airbnb that I was staying at. We pulled into a gated community. The security guard at the gate asked for my ID and name. A huge black gate slid open, and we pulled into the community. I frantically unloaded my luggage and went up an elevator into my room. It was a beautiful building that overlooked all of Downtown Kingston, with a sliding door out to a balcony view, where you could see the serene green hillsides and blue mountain peaks.

Now, I made a few calls and got in touch with a big time producer for dancehall artist "Popcaan." We scheduled a studio session where he would actually come to me and set up the studio right in my Airbnb.

During this trip, I desperately needed a mental break. Every morning, I would wake up, put on some instrumentals, roll up some weed, open a beer, and watch the sun rise into the sky. This was a routine for me, I spent this time reflecting, thinking, and praying. With every deep breath, I'd look out into the sky and just give God thanks for all he had done for me. I'd begun writing lyrics. Singing melodies over different beats and bouncing ideas off myself.

The day finally arrived when the producer came to my airbnb to set up. He pulled up in a blue Mark X. I excitedly rushed down the elevator to meet him. We transported all of his equipment in black louboutin luggage. As soon as we reached up stairs, we began to record right away.

After our session, he asked me how long have I been recording? I told him that I just got started. He responded and told me that I had no idea how gifted I was, but I needed to spend more time honing my craft. I appreciated his advice and validation that I was indeed talented.

I spent a few more days in Jamaica after my studio session, spending time with a friend. Now this friend knew a lot of people, one of who happened to be a videographer. I decided to hang out with them for the day. I met a lot of famous Jamaican artists and DJ's who were in the business.

Tony Rebel, Pantason, Ding-Dong, Skillibeng just to name a few. My trip to Jamaica helped build my confidence and calm me down. I learned alot about music and the music business and rubbing shoulders with old stars and up and coming stars, which made me more confident. I knew I could hang with the likes of them. It normalized them for me, and I didn't idolize them, but I respected their hustle and grind.

Before leaving Jamaica, I decided to head over to a place in Portmore called Gaza. Now, I didn't personally know anyone in Gaza per say, but I knew people who knew people. A friend and I took a taxi there for a party that they were having. As we walked down the street, many people were looking at us from windows and front steps. We met up with someone, and he began to call everyone from the area around. As we approached introducing me as a big international artist.

Now, the producer who recorded me in my Airbnb lived in Portmore, and he had left an important wire. I called him to pick it up. When he rolled up, he asked me if I knew anyone who lived in this area, and I said no. His last words were a warning for me to be careful. I listened to his words as I walked back into the outside party.

I started to get an uneasy feeling in the pit of my stomach. Something wasn't right. I leaned over to my friend and asked her if she wanted to leave. I told her I didn't have a good feeling. To my surprise, she had the same exact feeling. We quickly, but non chantilly called our taxi. I didn't let anyone around me become the wiser. I kept smiling, taking pictures, even bursting open a few bottles of champagne. Once our taxi had arrived, we disappeared into the shadows.

It was time for me to come back to the States. After an eventful trip, I had now gotten the confidence I needed. I knew that I could navigate and socialize in rooms and places amongst the biggest and brightest. As I boarded the plane, I had a new perspective on life.

One of the things that stood out to me was sitting on top of Tony Rebels studio. Where many of the biggest names in reggae have stood. This was a place where some of the biggest songs were written as well. Artists like Peter Tosh, Gregory Issacs, Koffee, and even the late great Bob Marley all stood on that roof or in that studio.

There were a few mango trees surrounding the studio. All the trees leaned towards the studio, but this tree leaned right over the studio. The Mangos could easily be taken from the tree without any extra effort. Tony Rebel said this happens because trees lean towards positive energy. I took a very valuable lesson from this.

*"In life, you never have to go out of your way to receive, if you let your light shine, then positivity, love, kindness, everything that is good for you will not only lean towards you but will be drawn to you!" - LANGU*

# *LET'S UNPACK*

Hey everyone, thank you for choosing this book to speak to you. I chose to write this book for many reasons, but as you all know, The Langu is a lifestyle brand. The Langu is all about living the word of God and sharing it in creative ways. I decided to write this book in an atypical way. After every chapter, you'll have a moment to unpack. This will include various questions of reflection and topics to bring into bible study with friends or your family, but most importantly, every chapter will have a scripture and a prayer point.

> ➢ What are the dreams or visions God has given you?

> ➢ How did Covid affect your life?

> ➢ What was the reason God gave Joseph the dream?

*Proverbs 3:5 Trust in the LORD with all thine heart; And lean not unto thine own understanding.*

*Proverbs 3:6 In all thy ways acknowledge him, And he shall direct thy paths.*

- Heavenly Father, In the name of Jesus Christ of Nazareth, Teach me to trust in your understanding, I know you are in control of my life, I ask that you direct my path in all my endeavors, dreams, and visions.

# ESSENTIAL - LANGU

Say, Lord Speak to me and begin writing, or drawing by faith.

# Chapter 2

## HINDSIGHT - NO STRESS

Upon returning from Jamaica, something in me had been ignited. I sat in the blue chair, in the noisy Kingston airport terminal. Suddenly, I began to see, hear, and feel sounds in a different way. Without uttering a word, I grabbed my red iPhone and went over to YouTube. I typed in Afro-beats instrumentals and clicked the first instrumental I saw.

As the instrumental played through my white AirPods, I motioned my hands in front of me as if I were sitting behind a piano, I started to slowly press my fingers in the air as if I were to play an imaginary piano. I know to some, this may have seemed foolish, but somehow, the words began to flow in my mind.

"You ain't gotta stress, baby,

You ain't gotta stress"....

The lyrics flowed out of me as I thought about my situation back at home, all the arguments and stress that led me to this point, and the feeling of being overwhelmed and frustrated. I put them into the words, or better yet, I made the statement.

"You ain't gotta stress..."

I was talking to myself in these lyrics and expressing emotions through my delivery. Although I was in a situation of depression, and things appeared as if they were falling apart in my life, I kept telling myself not to stress.

By the time my plane landed and I arrived back in the States, I was super excited. I got off the plane and went to my silver Volkswagen and drove straight to a party. People were still wearing masks outside. Covid was still something that we as a world had to pay attention to. However, everyone and I reached a point where I believe we just wanted to enjoy life. We just wanted to desperately be happy.

When I arrived at the party, there was no more parking, so the ignorant side of me decided to make my own parking space. I parked right in front of a "No Parking" sign. I stepped out of my silver Volkswagen and headed towards the door. There was a long line at the entrance to this nightclub. Even though the party was ending in 20 minutes, I just had to get inside.

When I finally made it into the nightclub, I started to scan the party for my friends. It's no surprise that I found them near the bar. My friends were surprised to see me, I didn't tell anyone when I was coming back. I decided to order 3 bottles of champagne to celebrate my safe return and my new found mental state.

As the bartenders approached us with fire shooting out of the sparklers and bottles in their hands, all eyes were on our group. I mean, who orders bottles when the party is about to be over?

Within the next 10 minutes, the party was over. We only opened two bottles and barely drank them all. It was now midnight, but none of us wanted to go home. We decided to drive to a random hotel parking lot just to hang out. Luckily, my car was still in the no parking spot in front of the club. I quickly got in my vehicle and drove off. All of us drove to this parking lot and started trying to finish drinking the rest of the bottles. Of course, as black people, we played our music from our cars really loudly.

The night was still young, the stars were twinkling, you could hear the sound of crickets chirping in the bushes near our cars, and the nighttime breeze was refreshingly keeping us cool on a warm summer night. For that entire summer, the artist I had been around created this routine that we would always do.

We would play instrumentals and sing, rap, or what we like to call it in Jamaica, DJ our songs on the beats. No matter the tempo or key, you would have to try and deliver your best performance. This exercise sharpened our ability to adjust and be versatile, no matter what was playing.

In the midst of us having a good time, one of the artists wanted to hand me their phone. I questioned him as to why and who was on the phone? He proceeded to show me the phone screen and answered and said," It's my father." He started to explain that this was a man from Africa whom he's been consulting and listening to in hopes that he can get him rich.

He wanted me to also speak with this man. Suddenly, that same feeling I had in Jamaica when I wanted to leave the party early came over me again. This was a friend of a friend who allowed me to meet with some people in Gaza back in Portmore, Jamaica.

## *"I sternly told him no, I don't want to speak with anyone and asked him if he could never ask me something like that again." - LANGU*

The night ended shortly after that; I didn't get home until about 2 a.m that morning. In regular Tony Tyme fashion, I poured a little Moscato into a wine glass and began listening to more beats. I lived in a two-bedroom apartment. It had a kitchen, a living room dining room, and a small bathroom. In the living room, I had a blue sofa set with blue and orange pillows, a white TV stand with a fireplace with blue L.E.D lights on the side, and a black & white gaming chair set up.

Despite the size and everything that filled the rooms, I still felt empty. My apartment at the time was a reminder of all the pain I was feeling in the moment. The mother of my first children at the time took them and left. She would periodically come back, we would get into another argument, and she would leave again. This was a never-ending cycle.

This particular time, I hadn't seen my daughter in months. Despite my best efforts, nothing I had done seemed to work. However, listening to beats and creating melodies and hooks was like therapy for me. This helped my mind focus and helped calm my nerves.

I kept reaffirming and telling myself not to give up. I found solace and purpose in creating. My peer and I decided to put together a live show, we would call it "Fyah Live Experience." Basically, all that we had been doing all year was practice, it was gearing us up to showcase what we had been working on. Simply going live from our phone and inviting a few friends. When the night finally came, it was an amazing event.

As we performed our songs live across social media, we garnered a lot of attention and support. One in particular would be an artist manager. Now, this artist manager loved the event and wanted to partner with us to do it again with more artists. I thought it was a great idea, so I called the other artists who helped plan the first one, and they agreed to do it again.

This artist manager began introducing me to other artists and producers. Upon meeting various like-minded artists, one particular producer was very interested in working with me. After sitting with him for a few days and getting to know him on a professional level, I could see that he was a very talented engineer and songwriter.

I never had any ego, I was always a person who was willing to learn, even if it meant learning things I already knew. This is Langu I like to call "Downward Learning." Now, this took patience. I would sit in the studio many nights just listening, watching, and learning. Soaking up information.

I love the studio, I love watching others in their element, doing what makes them happy. It was a privilege to witness creative individuals at work. Eventually, this music manager, the producer, and I sat many nights in the studio talking about music, life, and many stories about the music industry.

Now, the studio was very Islandy, it had guitars on the wall, two small sofas, wood floors, a custom desk for the computer, and recording equipment. As well as a fully acoustically treated recording booth.

One day, I decided it was time to record. I called the producer to see when I could come and record a song that I felt like I needed to express. He told me that he had been waiting to record with me and that I should come that night.

I walked into the studio very nervous that night. My stomach was in knots. He asked me if I had the beat that we would be working on, and I said yes. After everything was loaded up, I very calmly walked into the dark, hot, studio booth. I remember there was a small glass window I could look out from to see the engineer.

My palms were sweating like I just dipped my hand in a bucket of water. My heart was pounding like the hooves of a race horse in a Kentucky derby. I placed the black headphones on my head. Carefully adjusting the sizing to fit my rather large head.

Then, I did something out of the ordinary, something I'd never done before. I told the engineer to play the beat, and let it play. As the beat played through the black headphones neatly resting over my ears, I began to pray. I petitioned God, if he would help me right here, in this studio booth, that, once I accomplished this desire of becoming what others said I couldn't be, then I would use my voice to serve him. I would return to preaching and winning souls for his kingdom,

I asked him to use me and my music as a way to show others the way to him. Before finishing up my prayer, I recited Matthew chapter 6, "The Lords Prayer." You see, I already knew God had a calling on my life, and I understood and believed he would answer my prayer.

## *"I said Amen with all belief that I was connected to Christ." - LANGU*

17

When I opened my eyes, I knew I was ready. I signaled the engineer to restart the beat. As the beat played over again through the headphones, I began to play an imaginary piano, then I began to sing those same lyrics from the airport.

"You ain't gotta stress baby, You ain't gotta stress,

Anytime you wanna flex, you know the vibe

when I slide on you".

Now, the lyrics to my song had nothing to do with Jesus, the Church, or Christianity, but I believe the holy spirit gifted me a unique ability that night. I sounded like a whole new person. As I sang the words to the song and reached the chorus. I sang a melody I already knew, and I saw as the engineer sat up in his chair, He looked over at me and said, "I think you have something here, are you ready to record the song?"

By the time I finished recording, the engineer had taught me where to harmonize and where to add various dimensions to my vocals so that the song came to life. When I looked out of that tiny window from the booth, I saw a face looking back at me. Faces of people who weren't in the studio when I started recording.

People started to come into the studio, hear me recording this song, and call others to the studio. By the time I finished recording, and came out of the booth, the studio was filled with people in awe of what we had just created.

Everyone in the studio at that present moment began to question me. I was riddled with questions, like where I had been all this time? Some even began to tell me that I had a unique and rare talent and voice.

The engineer told me that this was a really good song, and he liked the way it was created. We stood in front of the studio door, and he said to me, "I will be a big artist in the world, but I have to want it."

I have to be ready for what would come with having a talent and gift like this. I have to be ready even if this would cause me to be liked, hated, or compromised. I told him I was

18

more than ready for whatever and I wouldn't need to compromise.

The studio session was very exciting. When I finally got back home that night, I was filled with excitement. I sat on my blue sofa and felt an overwhelming feeling of Joy. I played the song about a thousand more times, listening to hear what I could change or add to it in order to make it better. I still wasn't satisfied with just one song.

I went to bed that night and had an interesting series of dreams. I dreamt that one of the brothers of an artist I had been working with came to the studio and accused me of shining too bright. He was upset that I was getting all the attention and thought that his brother deserved it more than me.

He blamed the engineer, and then he blamed me. He stormed out of the studio, and then I saw a pot of soup. Then I saw someone or something seemingly putting something in the soup. The dream switched a few moments later to someone coming into the studio and offering me that same soup.

I then saw myself wearing a golden shirt while standing in the studio, then the dream shifted to an enormous warehouse, with multiple floors. At the top of the warehouse, there was a room and a ladder that took you into a studio that was located at the pinnacle of the warehouse.

The engineer sat there and said am I ready, I told him that I would be right back. I went outside of the warehouse. I could see hundreds of people swarming the warehouse, some looking to kill me. I began to run through the warehouse, which had multiple rooms that appeared to be of different types of temptations, all while there was like one big party going on.

As I was chased and running for my life, I made my way through various obstacles and close calls back up to the top of that warehouse. I finally made it into the room with the engineer, and I closed and locked the hatch that was on the floor under me.

*"I woke up that morning a little confused. It had been a while since I had a dream; to be honest, it had been a while since I prayed." - LANGU*

As I laid in bed a while, my phone began to ring, news began spreading of my studio session and my new song. For the first time, people who never paid me any mind or attention began to believe in me.

The artist manager called me, and we spoke about the song and plans for it. I asked him if he would help manage me as an artist. He asked me if I was sure, and I said yes. We planned to shoot a music video, and everything started moving very quickly from this point.

I began going to the studio more and more, spending most of my time in the studio. One day, the artist with whom I had been working came into the studio with his brother. He started to call out the engineer, telling him that he wanted to be the one to work with him. Then someone walked through the door and said they had just made some soup and offered me some to drink.

*"Remember what you asked God for; it might surprise you how many times he's answered you." - LANGU*

*The Creative way God speaks to you and through you.*

# LET'S UNPACK

➢ Have you ever been in a situation to compromise what you believe in?

➢ How often do you pray for help?

➢ What was the reason God gave Joseph the dream?

*Jeremiah 29:13 You will seek me and find me when you seek me with all your heart.*

*Psalms 23:5 Thou preparest a table before me in the presence of mine enemies; Thou anointest my head with oil; my cup runneth over.*

• Heavenly Father, In the name of Jesus Christ of Nazareth, Show me how to seek you with my entire heart, show me your face, show up in my life, bless me in the presence of my enemies, bless and anoint my mind, thoughts, and visions. Fill my cup, oh lord, until it overflows.

# ESSENTIAL - LANGU

Say, Lord Speak to me and begin writing, or drawing by faith.

# Chapter 3

# HINDSIGHT CLUBHOUSE PROPHECY

After having such a successful record that everyone loved, I decided to utilize my skills from my party promotion days. I began promoting the record everywhere to everyone. I was on an app called "ClubHouse" every day, sometimes for hours. I met a lot of people on that app from the music industry. People like Radio DJs, Producers, Record Execs, Artists, Song Writers.

I started a viral trend on the clubhouse app called "My Toxic Traits." Where people talked about their toxic traits, red flags, and many other things in hopes of promoting healing. It eventually turned into weeks long conversations, and a lot of people just needed community.

After raising my clubhouse following, I was now connected with people from all over the world. In various industries, doctors, lawyers, artists, music execs, and radio DJs. I got really hooked on the app and started joining other rooms that had similar interests to mine.

NewYear's eve rolled around, and I decided to head over to the studio. A Lot of people came by the studio that night before they went out to party. I personally didn't have any plans, things had still been really rocky at home, although I had 2 children, but because my relationship with their mom ended, it left me in a state of depression.

I had mixed emotions, but ultimately, I just felt all alone. I finally understood why some people didn't like the holidays. It's a reminder to most people of the family that they lost or never had.

I sat in the studio that night recording myself, ideas that I had been working on that I wanted to eventually lay down. I used to do this many nights, often teaching myself how to engineer myself, mostly, it was just a place where I could escape the emptiness of my apartment. I watched as the clock struck midnight, I poured myself a glass of wine, and began to indulge in some drinking. Then I got that funny feeling again. That same feeling that I got in Jamaica, the same feeling I got when my friend tried to hand me the phone.

Something was telling me to leave the studio. I decided to stay just a few more hours. Eventually, I finally called it a night at around 2 AM; however, I still had that funny feeling. At the time, I wasn't driving, so I had to call an M cab to pick me up. Luckily, there was one in the area, and it came rather quickly. As I walked out of the studio on that cold January morning.

I remember the crisp, cold air hitting my face as I stepped out of the studio door. I quickly closed it behind me, and I ran through the side of the house past all the snow that had fallen days before. I got into the silver and green M cab, and the driver asked me if my name was "Anthony" to be sure he picked up the right person.

As he accelerated away from the snowy curb and we pulled off away from the studio, a car came speeding down the street and turned erratically onto the street we just left, the cab was turning right as I saw a car filled with guys dressed in all black with black masks.

They stopped their car in the middle of the street as the cab turned. The driver seemed confused and nervous, as neither he nor I knew what was going on. I will never forget this moment because it seemed like the world was moving in slow motion. So slow that I got a good look into the eyes of one of the boys in the backseat of the car.

I looked behind me as the car made a U-turn and went back up the street the way they came. I knew that that car was filled with people coming to the studio because they knew that I was there. I'm not sure what was the reason, I'm not sure who sent them, I'm not even sure who they were, but I knew they were sent for me.

I kept looking behind the car to see if anyone was following. When I finally got home, I didn't go to sleep. I walked through the front door and, through the keys on the table, turned the fireplace on. I plopped down in my black and white gaming chair. I guess you could say that this was my thinking chair, it was in this chair that I created and decompressed.

I unlocked my phone and went to the clubhouse app. I scrolled until I found a room called prophetic night. I entered the room with no expectations. I just wanted to listen. The room wasn't that filled with too many people when I entered.

There was gospel music playing in the background, and a man by the name of Jeremiah was talking. He began to call people up to the platform and said that he would start ministering soon. Just then, he started to speak into the lives of different people. Suddenly, out of the blue, he randomly called my name.

Now, I was very skeptical at the time however, I listened with an open mind. He called my name and began to tell me that The Lord was calling me, he began to say that I went through many things as a child, which was a plan by the enemy to shut up my emotions and stop me from feeling and that God was getting ready to heal me.

He then said that he saw me on many different stages and asked me if I was a speaker. I told him that I was an artist, and he said that God was getting ready to elevate me to multiple spheres of influence and to do things that people never thought I would be able to do.

He told me that I would begin to walk confidently in what God called me to do. He told me that the genre of music that

I was doing wasn't the genre that he hears but I was mixing different sounds together.

He told me that there were certain people who had just entered my life that were sent to diminish my value, some women and some men, and I had to be careful of who was around me. He told me that the lord was sending a strong spirit of might.

Was he indeed a prophet of God? I believed in God and that he was indeed speaking to me. So, I took this word and held on to it as a confirmation that God heard my prayers. Although I took this word and focused on only certain parts of it I didn't fully understand the word. I recorded what he was saying to me and took it to God in prayer.

## *"I was reminded of a dream I had years prior." - LANGU*

I had also received many prophetic words throughout the years, some of which were often very vague. It was as if God didn't want to reveal who I was to everyone but would only show them glimpses.

I was often told that I was going places, but I had to seek God. I was often told that I was very special and a different type of child. I was told that I was God's mouthpiece and an oracle of God.

For some reason, this Clubhouse experience reminded me of those prophetic words. I had drifted away from God so much that I forgot what God said about me.

The next day, I went to the studio and shared the prophetic word with my manager. I remember expressing to him that I needed to maneuver smartly because I couldn't trust anyone around me. The thing I always kept private was who I was prior to this moment. No one knew my relationship with God ran as deep as it did.

I was very transparent with my manager, and I knew that God had graced me to do what I was doing, so I didn't have any fear moving forward. I knew I would make it if I continued to put the work in. I kept working diligently over the course of the next couple of months.

My notoriety grew as I worked with my manager and various producers. The way I viewed everyone around me changed. I began to pay more attention. No one around me understood or knew the relationship I had with God. I never shared the fact that I was a dreamer. I would tell others that I believe in God because I have a personal relationship with him.

*The Creative way God speaks to you and through you*

# LET'S UNPACK

➢ Have you ever been in a situation to compromise what you believe?

➢ How often do you pray for help?

➢ What was the reason God gave Joseph the dream?

*Jeremiah 29:13 You will seek me and find me when you seek me with all your heart.*

*Psalms 23:5 Thou preparest a table before me in the presence of mine enemies; Thou anointest my head with oil; my cup runneth over.*

- Heavenly Father, In the name of Jesus Christ of Nazareth, Show me how to seek you with my entire heart, show me your face, show up in my life, bless me in the presence of my enemies, bless and anoint my mind, thoughts, and visions. Fill my cup, oh lord, until it overflows.

# ESSENTIAL - LANGU

Say, Lord Speak to me and begin writing, or drawing by faith.

# Chapter 4

# HINDSIGHT - RUN

## RUNNING FROM A FEELING

I reached a point on my journey where I started to do great things. Opportunities started coming my way. Many people finally recognized and noticed my work. Seemingly, I tried to make sure everyone around me was happy and enjoying themselves. Never complaining about my hardships and my problems; I tried to make everything appear to be great.

Life started moving very fast for me, I was living fast. Drinking, smoking, sex, parties. A lot of late nights, early mornings, the days begin to blur together. I was always either high or drunk, most days both. I fully embodied this persona, this made up identity, "TheTonyTyme."

I had completely lost my way, I lost my identity and who I was. Things aren't always as they appear. I literally became a new person. However, I was very unhappy, the weight of missing my children. All the things I endured growing up and held inside, all the things I was still enduring, became unbearable. I started masking the pain with vices, These vices only served as temporary band-aids.

I always felt alone, like things were mundane. I felt like everything was grey. I tried to find various things, all in the pursuit of "Making It" and proving everyone who ever doubted me wrong. I began traveling a lot more in hopes of escaping my reality.

With no money or plan, I flew to various places like Miami, New York, and even Jamaica. I was spiraling downward, even if it appeared I was rising in music. I was imprisoned by my bad habits, by my traumatic past, and the persona of being "The life of the party."

To add on to this already out of control dilemma, one day, on a Thanksgiving morning. I decided to pack up all my clothes into two suitcases. I confronted my mom, who had been speaking with me about paying the rent money I owed her, and I just told her I was leaving and heading for Atlanta.

She looked at me with a puzzled disposition. Worried and concerned, she never truly believed in music or that dream of mine. She never understood any of it. Despite others telling her how successful I would become, she was looking for tangible evidence she had bills to pay, I had bills to pay, too.

Before I left, I decided to visit a very close friend whom I actually consider family. When I entered her house, I didn't smell the usual smell of thanksgiving. I sat amongst them and wanted to know what the thanksgiving plans were.

I began feeling like no one wanted me around, no one cared about me. No one asked me how I was doing. It felt like I was just giving and giving, and the more I tried to replenish myself I couldn't. I couldn't because others needed my high energy.

I told them my goodbyes, jumped in my white BMW X3 at around noon, and decided to drive to Atlanta by myself. No job, No money, literally just a dollar and a dream. I GPS'd Atlanta, Georgia, got on I-91 South, and put the pedal to the metal.

At the time, I had a friend who really believed in me. She once told me that if I ever needed anything, she would be there. She told me that the least she can do for me is make sure I eat every day.

I was so filled up with pride at the time, but truth be told, I needed the help. I spent years struggling to eat, or eating too little, I developed extreme acid-reflux because I would go days without a decent meal, with just weed and liquor in my system.

This friend began to send me money every week. she said to me, "At least get something to eat.". Still, to this day, unbeknown to her, this broke my pride issues.

I drove all day and night. I remember at the time, comedian Kevin Hart just released a new comedy special on Netflix. I watched it as I drove on the not so busy highways. When that ended, I listened to music, I smoked weed, I drank liquor. Eventually, after driving all day, I finally arrived in Atlanta, I only knew one person who lived there.

I called him up and asked him if I could stay at his house for a few days. He was so gracious and excited to see me after not seeing each other in years. It turned out that he would oblige.

The perception that most people had of me was that I had already made it. I was everywhere, always smiling and laughing, coming with high energy. Most people didn't know I had a fake diamond chain I bought from a website to look the part.

## *"Confidence is key" - LANGU*

I begin telling this friend my entire truth. The prophecy, I told him that I believe God was going to come through for me. I begin to tell him that anything in his life that he needs or wants, he just has to choose God. I was preaching to him.

While on this trip, I reached out to someone I knew and got the opportunity to record at the same studio, rapper "Young Thug" records at. I was in talks with a VP of a popular record label. They began to talk with me about growing my audience and signing me to eventually present me to a major record label.

While in that studio, I was able to engineer myself, I sat in the studio and started to write a song entitled "Love Langu." It was my first time in a multi-million dollar studio. I felt like I was so close to making a career out of music. Here, I was in a brand new city for the first time and found my way into a record label studio. This inspired me and also made what I had been chasing seem obtainable. Music was no longer a dream, but it became a goal, it became work.

After my studio session, I still wanted to record something else. I reached out to someone else whom I knew. They instructed me to head over to another studio with a long time friend. I jumped on I-85 and headed to a place called Stone Mountain. When I arrived at the studio, I pulled into a parking lot where there was a car dealership. A man came out to greet me and took me around the back, where they had a full studio setup. It wasn't big, but it felt like Jamaica.

I saw pictures of Sizzla hanging on the wall, Gucci mane, and many more artists. I was again in another hidden gem, a studio with a lot of history. A few hours later, to my surprise, the infamous producer "Delly Ranks" appeared in the studio. —· He heard me sing one time, pulled me away from everyone, and told me that I was different and I had a special gift.

## *"He said there is something that is in me, and once I tap into that, I would be great." - LANGU*

Eventually, I had to leave the friend's house where I was lodging at. His mom just couldn't have me there, sleeping on the floor with no money, no job, just free loading. I understood, and I was just grateful for the short amount of time she allowed me to be there.

Unfortunately, I had to leave Atlanta after this. However, I made great connections and had a great experience. I returned to Connecticut with a greater belief. I knew I could achieve what I was dreaming of if I worked hard enough.

Upon returning, I started to meet new people. New producers, new artists, and because I had just come back from Atlanta I was the hottest thing in my mind.

I began coming to the realization that the people around

31

me were treating me differently. In studio sessions, I noticed a lot of whispering. I, in return, pretended to be high all the time just to listen to their conversations. I told them that I started taking mushrooms. However, in these moments, I begin getting that feeling in my gut again. Something was brewing, something in my spirit was uneasy.

I decided to run and venture back to Atlanta again. Not for nothing, I was receiving divine favor left, right, and center. Producers, engineers, and artists all wanted to work with me. Sometimes, they just liked me to be around in the studio as they created, they said that it was spiritual.

Truth is, I always felt like I didn't deserve any of this however, I was grateful to be receiving it. So, I booked a flight to Atlanta. A popular record producer and businessman wanted me to record some music with him as well as write some music for other artists. When I landed in Atlanta the second time, I reached out to another friend to stay with for a couple of days.

She was gracious enough to welcome me into her space with open arms. While there, I began to open up to her, I told her all that I was currently battling. She was taken back and shocked because of how I portrayed myself on social media and in the eyes of the public.

## *"I told her the ups people see on social media don't always reflect the downs we go through." - LANGU*

I began to tell her about my relationship with God. Our friendship was plutonic. I was sleeping on her sofa, and the lord used me to encourage her. However, the present dangers that I faced were very real. I began to grow very afraid for my life.

However, there is only one reason I was able to survive anything, and that was because I knew God was with me. I explained to her that since a child, I was able to understand things that most people didn't. I knew a woman of God by the name of Pastor Joycelyn. She spoke a word into my life, telling me not to compromise and that I was going places.

Just as we finished our conversation, my phone rang, and it was Pastor Joycelyn. We spoke for a little, but she told me that I needed to be careful. She said I needed to ask God's permission to go places and to do anything. I had to be careful who I ate and drank from and where I went.

At this moment, I understood exactly what she meant because of all the gut feelings I kept getting since Jamaica. Although I was receiving these feelings, I decided to run. The truth is I was running from everything and everyone. Although I didn't know what I did wrong, I couldn't shake the feeling of being afraid. Terrified to allow anyone to get close to me, terrified to trust, terrified to love, and terrified of being around too many people at one time.

Being in Atlanta gave me a fresh perspective, but also made me afraid to be around people. I started to understand the weight of favor.

*"The thing about receiving favor is that there will always be people around you who feel like you are not deserving."*

*- LANGU*

*The Creative way God speaks to you and through you*

# LET'S UNPACK

➢ What are you running from?

➢ Do you ask God permission?

➢ Can you still trust God, even when things go wrong in your life?

**Romans 10:17** So then faith cometh by hearing, and hearing by the word of God.

**Jonah 1:3** Jonah immediately tried to run away from the Lord by going to Tarshish. He went to Joppa and found a ship going to Tarshish. He paid for the trip and went on board. He wanted to go to Tarshish to get away from the Lord.

- Heavenly Father, In the name of Jesus Christ of Nazareth, Teach me how to trust your word, Increase our faith in you, forgive us for running away from what you called us to do, Father, reveal our assignments and give us strength and understanding when the time comes to complete them.

# ESSENTIAL – LANGU

Say, Lord, Speak to me and begin writing, or drawing

by faith.

# Chapter 5

# HINDSIGHT - FAVOR IN MY LOWEST

One day, I received a phone call to accompany another artist to perform a show. Now, this show opportunity was opening up for Reggae Dancehall superstar Sean Paul. These opportunities always happened because I was in the right places at the right time.

## *"There is power in location" - LANGU*

It seemed like everything I had been working for finally began to manifest. Subsequently, these things were happening at my lowest point in life, in my mind, and in my spirit.

I was held captive by the vices that I decided to use to cope. These vices had a hold on me, I was addicted to them to alter my state of mind, and numb my reality. Yet still, I was fully functioning and ambitious and hungry, ready to take on any challenge.

I was still wrestling with my identity. However, I understood and wholeheartedly believed that God was with me. I felt that if I just remained close to him, everything would be alright.

The night before the show, I was feeling nervous, thinking about all that I had been through to reach this point. I began to cry, and eventually, that turned into me praying. While

35

praying, I could see myself on the stage, meeting Sean Paul, I saw myself in the room, and everything went well. As I finished praying, I asked for protection and guidance as I ventured into performing.

The day came for the show, The feeling of excitement filled my mind. Can you imagine being at your lowest point in life, caught up in depression and facing obstacles everyday, but yet receiving unbelievable opportunities. I was overcome with various emotions, nervous but ready at the same time.

I carefully picked out my outfit as the show was about an hour and half away from Hartford. I loaded up my car with a few other artists, and we took to the road. I made sure to bring a few glasses from my brand. I just launched "The Langu." I had to make sure that I left a lasting impression. The Langu was something that I created one late night while staying up thinking in my thinking chair.

We drove up to the college music hall in New Haven, Connecticut. It's a popular place where some of the biggest artists in the world perform. When we got there, it was early. We had to do a sound check and see the dressing rooms. We walked up the front stairs of the music hall. When we entered through the wooden doors we stood inside just looking at an empty room. I got this overwhelming feeling like all the hard work and sacrifices I put in could actually pay off one day. I felt like I was exactly where I was meant to be.

We went through a side hall down some more stairs to the dressing rooms, there was a sign on the door that listed out the artists names, however, the sign didn't have me labeled as an artist, but instead, it had me labeled as a DJ. Someone made the comment about that and wanted me to bring it up to the venue, however, I consider those details very small. I was grateful to just be in the room.

## *"When it's your moment to shine, expect the devil to show up"- LANGU*

A few hours passed by, we laughed and talked about the moment, just then, someone looked at me and asked me how

I was able to remain so calm. I told them that it was because I prayed about this day before the day even came. The fact that I was there wasn't in my own strength or power but because of the power and favor of God.

I took time to tell that person that anything you want in life, you just have to put God first and pray, and whenever you reach those answered prayers, do not be afraid, but know that God heard you and answered you. Continue to walk by faith. There I was preaching again, to a complete stranger at a Sean Paul show.

Shortly after it was show time, it went from an empty hall to a packed out hall. A couple of thousand people were all in the room to see Sean Paul perform.

We were the opening acts, I was completely okay if I didn't get to perform. I was just happy and grateful to be in the room. I had on black leather boots with a green trim, blue jeans, a black T-shirt, and a fur leopard print jacket. I was wearing my signature black Langu Shades with a golden lens and an iced out "TheTonyTyme" chain glistening from my neck.

When everyone saw me, they immediately asked, "Who is that?" You look like the star tonight, not the main artists who had invited me to perform. It made me feel uncomfortable, as I'm sure it made the main artist, too. I smiled and said thank you. I cheered as loud as I could for the other artists as they performed. I love seeing others in their element and shining. I was often told that for someone who had a huge following, I didn't act like a star, I acted like a regular person.

The moment came, they called me out on stage to perform. My heart was racing, palms sweating. Anytime I feel nervous, I know that it's a Langu moment. A moment of greatness. I danced my way onto the stage. I heard as the crowd erupted, and then I took the microphone and started to sing. At first, everyone was looking at me, wondering who I was. I heard a few people in the crowd singing the lyrics back to me.

# "CHEER FOR OTHERS, DON'T BECOME SO CONSUMED IN EGO AND PRIDE THAT YOU STOP BEING HUMBLE" - *LANGU*

When I started to sing "No Stress" that's when the crowd erupted with hundreds of screaming fans who just genuinely loved music. They screamed louder for me than they did for the artists who performed before me. It was like I was destined to be on that stage.

After I came off the stage, all my adrenaline was pumping. Everyone started to congratulate me and tell me that I had a big future in music. I stood by a door and just took a backseat, I wanted to remember the moment. The smell of weed smoke filled the air. The hennessy and champagne and all the people in the dressing room made the moment cinematic.

That's when a man I've never seen strolled by me. As he walked by, he looked at me and said, "You look like a star, who are you?" I told him my name, Then he said that I had the image of a superstar. He asked if I was the one singing those songs that opened the show, and I said yes.

Standing next to me was another artist, the one who invited me, the one who actually opened the show. It turned out this man was Sean Paul's best friend. He completely ignored the other artist, and for some reason, he focused on me. He asked me if I wanted to meet Sean Paul, and I said yes!

I actually had some glasses I brought to give to Sean Paul. He walked me through the smoke filled dressing room. We walked through these black doors, and brought me into a room. Inside the room, I saw Sean Paul face to face. He introduced me and said that I brought him a gift. I told him my name and said that I brought these LANGU glasses for him.

He took them and said "thank you" and went to try them on. He already had on palm angel glasses, and he took those off and realized my glasses matched his outfit perfectly. He asked the entire dressing room, "How mi look?" and everyone said, wow, they really like those glasses, they told him it matched his outfit perfectly.

He turned to me and asked, "Who are you?" I said I'm an artist, but also a businessman, a man of God, and us meeting like this is fate. This day was destined to happen, and you know that. He looked at me with a wide smirk and shook my hand. He said that he was going to perform in the glasses.

I stood there in the dressing room in awe of how much favor God was showing me. I never doubted for a second that it was God who allowed me into this room, it was God's glory that was being seen on me.

Even in a space where all types of things were taking place, God still showed me favor. I followed Sean Paul and his entourage out onto the stage, and I stood off to the side. I watched as the dancers went out, and the show started with the crowd screaming and shouting.

I remembered my childhood growing up listening to songs like "get busy" and many more and winning dance competitions at parties as a kid. I was extremely grateful to be there. As I stood there, I began to hear the hearts of people around me. It felt like the brightest light was shining on me, standing on the side of the stage.

Everyone is questioning 'Who is this?" Why don't we know him? As I did a two step on the side of the stage, I could hear people talking to the side of me. "Look at him, He's really a star," they said. I pretended like I couldn't hear and just kept enjoying the show. After the show, Sean Paul and his entourage invited me to come to the studio after they finished touring to work on some new music.

The night was amazing. I got into my car and drove home completely in awe. I knew that I was gifted, and this showed me that God truly gave me grace. I woke up the next day and went straight to the studio with the other artists from the show. Now, this artist's father is a big time promoter. From working with Bob Marley, Sean Paul Beres Hammond, you name it.

As I sat in the studio that night, his father told me that everyone was calling him asking him about me. He told me as long as I stayed under his son, I would become the next biggest thing. I really didn't want to hear that. However, I shook my head and took another sip of my Hennessy. We began to talk about God. The producer turned to me and said, "You know that you're a prophet, right?" You've been sent by God, and I like that you are humble and you won't let anyone change your mind. He told me that I'm special because I make music from a different place.

My lyrics aren't just lyrics but messages that will resonate with people. I looked at him and asked him how he knew that, and he responded because he's a prophet too. He begins to explain that it's the reason why his life has been so hard and why he has to go through so much, and it's why I'm going through so much. I smiled, finished my drink, and continued smoking my weed. I knew that he was indeed telling the truth, and God was only using him as a point of contact.

*"God uses you, and he can use others around you, sometimes we don't recognize it." - LANGU*

The Creative way God speaks to you and through you

# *LET'S UNPACK*

➢ Are you cheering for others?

➢ Have you dismissed others because you view them as less then?

➢ Are you able to ignore small things to see the larger picture?

**Jeremiah 29:13** You will seek me and find me when you seek me with all your heart.

**Psalms 23:5** Thou preparest a table before me in the presence of mine enemies; Thou anointest my head with oil; my cup runneth over.

• Heavenly Father, In the name of Jesus Christ of Nazareth, Show me how to seek you with my entire heart, show me your face, show up in my life, bless me in the presence of my enemies, bless and anoint my mind, thoughts, and visions. Fill my cup, oh lord, until it overflows.

# ESSENTIAL - LANGU

Say, Lord Speak to me and begin writing, or drawing by faith.

# Chapter 6

# HINDSIGHT – JUST IN TIME

The news was out there, I had performed with Sean Paul. Pictures of Sean Paul and I circulating on social media. In the entertainment industry, perception is everything. The perception was that I was the fattest rising artist in my area. At least amongst my co-workers.

However, I was still spiraling. I had no Job, no money. I broke open a savings Jar filled with pennies and started buying food from the dollar store. I was broke, but yet still I found a way to smoke and drink everyday. Still on the outs with the mother of my children. I was a functioning drug addict and alcoholic.

I was extremely depressed. I was crying without there being any tears falling from my face. Everything was bad in my life. I felt like I lost everything. I was stuck. However, that never stopped me from making music. Creating was the one thing that made me feel like I was alive.

I kept writing, I kept creating. I found myself reaching out to some people I met in the industry to just encourage them. That made me feel alive as well. It was good to know that even though I was at the worst time in my life, I could still tell someone about God and hold on to faith.

I started to distance myself from the people I was around. I couldn't tell them it was because I started having dreams about them. Dreams about them plotting against me, hunting me, hating me, and trying to hurt me. Instead of leaving things to chance, I distanced myself.

One day, I needed to record a song and reached out to a mentor and producer I knew. He was a really nice person, always smiling and always willing to help others. He was misunderstood, but I considered him a friend. He picked me up and drove me to the studio. He had a friend in the car with him. They started talking about war crimes and dictators.

Somehow, the conversation turned, and we started talking about God. They started to say that God wasn't real, and they hated anyone who talked about God.

They went as far as to say "F" Jesus Christ. That made my blood boil, and I rebuked him for saying that. We went up into the studio and just stopped talking about it. However, I started having a conversation in my head. I started to tell myself that I was just going to stay away and record by myself.

Just as we reached the studio room, I received a text on my phone. My white X3, which was in the repair shop, was ready. I decided to Uber to the repair shop instead of driving because we just paid for parking. The producer didn't like that.

However, I quickly left and went straight to pick up my car. Praying on the way there, I realized I couldn't allow whatever that was going on to stop me from completing what I set out to do. So I decided to go back. I went straight to the studio and went straight to recording. After we finished recording, I paid them and left.

I stayed home for a few days to process everything that was going on in my life. After spending time away from myself, I was trying to figure out my next moves. I had this morning routine, wake up, brush my teeth, pour a glass of Moscato and hennessy, roll a nice joint, and sit in my sunroom.

Around this time, I stopped sleeping in my bed because I convinced myself that I didn't deserve a bed. I purposely made myself suffer. This morning, as I sat in my chair and watched the sun rise, something was different. I saw a tv appear before my eyes. I wondered if I was hallucinating or dreaming. I

43

watched as my entire life flashed before my eyes on the TV.

However, I saw all the moments where God intervened in my life. This was the first time I heard the holy spirit in me speaking. Telling me that it was he who saved my life. I saw many moments where I was being set up to die or my demise was being planned, but every time, the plans failed. The holy spirit said to me that if I continued down this path, I would end up in jail or worse.

I begin to cry, all these memories of things I did in life that were sinful, and wrong came back into my mind. Some of the events I didn't remember that I did. I felt the weight of guilt, and shame, I was ashamed I allowed myself to do such unspeakable things. I not only hurt myself, but I also hurt others.

# *"HURT PEOPLE HURT PEOPLE"-*
## *LANGU*

I started to weep because I knew I had strayed so far away from God. The tears that I held inside for almost 2 years began to flow down my face. There I was, sitting in a room with the sun shining on me, weed in my hand, and hennessy on the table crying. I put the weed down and began to tell God how sorry I was. Sorry for going against his word, sorry for sinning, sorry for allowing my flesh to rule over me, sorry for abusing drugs and alcohol, sorry for forgetting who I was.

For the next 40 days, I stayed in that room, weeping and asking God to forgive me. I started to make phone calls, texts, dm's reaching out to people that I could remember I had hurt. I started to apologize, asking for forgiveness. Some people I was too ashamed to talk to on the phone, so I wrote them messages explaining a little, but mainly asking for forgiveness.

In these 40 days I thought long and hard. I was reminded about a mentor I had who was a pastor and had a studio in his church.

I started to remember how I would go to prayer and

fasting. I remembered the days I preached the word in church. I remember the promise I made to God when I first recorded "No Stress." I told God that I would use my platform to lead others to him. I was not doing that, I was doing the opposite of that, I was using the platform God gave me to get high and drunk and sleep with women.

I decided to pick up my cross and walk. I decided to follow Jesus Christ again. I needed Jesus because I knew the only other option was dying in sin. I started to read my bible again. I was still drinking and smoking, but I started reading the bible.

I propped my phone up in front of me, and while reading the word of God, I felt the need to share it. By the leading of that burning desire, I started preaching into my phone, making videos, and posting them online. I had to share how good God was to me.

After 40 days, I received a phone call from a producer. He asked me where I've been, because I kind of just fell off the face of the earth. I told him that I reconnected my relationship with God, and there were a lot of things going on that I didn't agree with. I couldn't afford to let anyone compromise my relationship with God.

He began to grow unsettled and told me that I shouldn't believe in God. He told me that I shouldn't believe in Jesus, and that I should believe in him instead. He said he sees the potential in me, and if I chose to serve Jesus instead of him, it would take me longer to reach my destination. He said that he could get me there faster. All I had to do was give up my belief in Jesus. I responded and told him.

*"It doesn't matter how long it takes or if I never get there, I will never not profess my love and belief in Jesus Christ of Nazareth." - LANGU*

He laughed and we both hung the phone up. I began to

remember the scripture in the bible where satan tempted Jesus in the wilderness. He offered Jesus all the kingdoms of the world only if he bowed down and worshipped him. Jesus refused him. I had to refuse this producer even though he was offering me something I wanted.

A day later, I received a phone call from that same woman of God, "Pastor Joycelyn." She told me that she was a pastor now, and she wanted to start having church services in the area. She said that she knows I know a few people, and if I could help her locate a place.

I knew that this was God because this couldn't be just by chance. I was eager to help, I needed something to do, and I wanted to please God. So, I started to make a few calls. After some calls, I finally located a possible place for service.

Initially, I was just contacted to help find a place, but I realized that the church needed someone to operate the media. I knew my way around a sound board and a camera. I was more than happy to be doing something for someone other than myself.

After a few months of serving the church in the background, I was still struggling with smoking. I was broken hearted. Still dealing with a lot of personal issues. One day, I confessed to the pastor that I was struggling. She looked at me and said, "It's okay." The next time I tried to smoke, it made me feel sick. So, I completely quit and stopped smoking.

Fathers day was approaching, and then pastor Dr. Joycelyn came to me one day after church and said the lord said that she should put me up there to preach.

I laughed, because there's no way she knew I used to preach as a child. That was the part of me that I was hiding. I felt unworthy to speak in church. However, anything that the lord says for me to do I'm always inclined to be obedient. I knew that it was God who saved my life.

I knew that it was God who placed me in this church. It was on this day that the members of the church started to see what God placed in me. One of the members told me that God told them to pray for me because I was a pastor. Now, I really

46

don't subscribe to titles.

I'm just happy to be a part of God's children. Slowly but surely, I began to grow in the ministry. I kept reading my bible, praying, and studying the word—more than I have ever done in my entire life.

My life took a 180 turn. I was able to break my addictions. I started to walk in what God placed before me. It seemed so small, but yet this took me from a low place. This caused a change in my life. I started to view the world and life differently. God showed up for me "Just in Time." He used someone whom I already knew to show me that whatever God placed in me was greater than I imagined. All that I was chasing and running from was just a part of the journey.

The Creative ways God speaks to you and through you

# *LET'S UNPACK*

- ➢ Have you ever repented?

- ➢ Are you willing to cheer for others?

- ➢ Are you willing to stand up for Jesus?

**Matthew 4:10** Then said Jesus unto him, "Get thee hence, Satan! For it is written: 'Thou shalt worship the Lord thy God, and Him only shalt thou serve.

**Matthew 23:11-12** The greatest among you will be your servant. For those who exalt themselves will be humbled, and those who humble themselves will be exalted.

- • Heavenly Father, In the name of Jesus Christ of Nazareth, Teach me to be humble, teach me how to serve others. Lead me on a path of righteousness, keep me away from evil, never let me serve anyone or anything other than you, lord God, teach me how to discern evil to stay away from sinning against you.

# ESSENTIAL - LANGU

Say, Lord Speak to me and begin writing, or drawing by faith.

# Chapter 7

# HINDSIGHT - THE DREAM LINE

As a dreamer and someone who God has given a dream or vision. I didn't fully understand all that it entailed. The dream line is the journey of a dreamer. My journey came with a tremendous amount of downfalls. Sometimes, during my journey, I questioned God. Why me?

While walking my journey, I now understand that every down was a setup for a rise. The journey isn't told to the dreamer or the visionary. The journey is based on your actions. The journey is based on your faith. To reach great heights, it takes great faith.

I began to realize that the downs are actually moments of building character and potential. The deeper you go in God, the higher you'll be elevated. The depths of God can be a scary place because you have to surrender your desire for control.

On my journey, I witnessed many things. I met a multitude of people, some believers and some we would consider them sinners. As I read the word of God more, I came to understand that it was God who allowed anything and everything to happen to me.

*"When you realize that nothing just happens and God has a plan for your life, you begin to find strength in weak moments." - LANGU*

You find the strength to forgive when everything says you shouldn't. You find the strength to choose God even when every fiber of your being says otherwise. When you are walking the dream line, it's only by grace. The paths can make one become more rigid and judgmental. However, in my calling and what God chose to use me to be, I had to overcome that. I had to see life through different lenses to be able to see from multiple angles and dimensions.

## *"The Journey gives you definition and substance." - LANGU*

As a dreamer, it's important to know who God is, so that when you struggle with your identity, you'll be able to remember who's image you are created in. My journey taught me what I am capable of.

## *"My journey taught me that I might have to endure in order to soar."- LANGU*

I had to go through seasons of being betrayed, hurt, and seasons of feeling afraid. I had to go through seasons of bondage and depression. These are all stepping stones that you will face on the dream-line. I had to go through seasons where I couldn't find a familiar face, seasons where I felt like everyone hated me, and seasons where I couldn't find any familiar face to believe in me.

## *"Seasons where my independence was stripped away, and I had to depend on God." - LANGU*

This gives substance to when I preach, and I say, "If it had not been for the lord God on my side, where would I be?" I can say that and draw from my experiences along the dream line.

I can tell the aspiring dreamer or visionary that in the thick of things, trust in God, and he will see you through. He didn't bring you this far just to bring you this far, but God has a plan for you. It's not my job as a servant to tell you how to get to where God is bringing you, but I can strengthen you in your understanding and sights.

"The deeper you get into prayer, fasting, and the word of God, that is the higher you will soar. There is no way that I could have understood this while in my seasons of Down. When God has hand selected you, your life isn't going to be easy. In part, you aren't going to make your life easy.

You can't speed the process up either. Your choices created some of your issues. The things I faced were because of what was in my heart and what I allowed to be in my heart.

Dreamers and visionaries have the great responsibility of forgiving and serving those who have hurt them. I sat for weeks, maybe months, and spent time asking for forgiveness. When I reached everyone I could think of, I still didn't reach myself.

The responsibility of connecting with God is to make sure you do the work on self. Before feeding God's people. This is something that takes introspection. As a person who uses words to reach others, I never want those words to come from a corrupted, biased, hurt, or shameful place. I want to make sure I'm pouring from a clean cup.

Even in the aspects of writing and releasing music, and how that impacted my lifestyle. When I was searching for something, I could only find it in Christ.

Once I reconnected to Christ, I realized what God desired of me. While I never desired ministry, working for God, and serving others in the capacity of declaring God's word, which is what he placed in me. Sometimes, we can become so blinded by worldly views that we miss what is right in front of us. We miss what is inside of us because we rely on the world more than we rely on God.

Being able to hear from God, see from God, and speak from God isn't just an everyday thing. It's something that is given with the expectation that it will be used for others. It's something that you have to nourish, and nurture. It's something you have to cultivate and protect.

Having a relationship with God isn't something you'll have to broadcast. The proof is in the pudding. It is impossible to truly have a relationship with God, and someone isn't able to discern that.

What others were identifying in me was confirming what God was already telling me. Telling me through dreams, through feelings, through conviction, through people. I may have had desires to just become an artist and make music and be on stages singing and performing, but God had bigger plans for me.

God had a different desire for me. The stage I would be on wasn't one to perform my own words, but it was to declare the words that he placed in me.

The various prophetic words that I received were just mere glimpses. It's only a part of God's plan being revealed so that I can move in faith.

## *"It's vital to read the word of God so that you can gain knowledge and understanding."- LANGU*

Walking the dream line means that you're walking in the spirit because whatever dream or vision God gave you is going to take faith. It's going to take you trusting God despite of what others say, despite what you see, and despite when you don't see. It's this type of trust that will ultimately keep you.

The question is, "Is God Enough?" When you can answer this with a yes, then your seasons of "Down" become seasons of "Potential." They become the seasons of building and preparation, they become the seasons of seeking, they become the seasons where you exercise your faith and serve others despite what's going on in your life. The way to see God in your life is to sometimes go back and see where he took you from and see where and how far you've come. This isn't to dwell on the past, but it's to see where God's hands were in your life.

Sometimes, as you're living through it, you don't always recognize the hand of God. We like to say we face adversity and problems, and we often blame it on the devil. When you take time to really ask God for understanding, you'll realize that all along, God allowed it.

God allowed them to betray you, God allowed you to take that road, God allowed you to feel alone, God allowed you to take those drugs, God allowed you to make those mistakes.

The reason why God allows these things is not for your downfall, but it's all about your rise. It's so that when he finally elevates you, when you finally reach where you're supposed to be. You'll be able to look back and grasp the fact that you didn't do it by yourself.

You'll be able to serve those whom God loves even when you aren't 100% where you want to be. You'll be able to show love and kindness and mercy. The same grace that was given to you after you made a mistake. It is the same grace you should give to others.

There are many reasons why we stay in certain seasons of "down," but one of the most common is that we refuse to let it go and let God. As a man of faith, I realized that all along, I had been trying to do things my way. I had been trying to accomplish things based on my knowledge and my understanding. I never once just let go and let God.

The moment that I got reconnected, I was broken. I had no choice but to "let go and let God." I reached a place where I knew that the only way is YHWH. Walking the dreamline isn't for the faint of heart. However, I can surely and boldly declare that all things are possible through Christ Jesus. When you reach that level of dependency in God, that is when doors begin to open up.

Don't lose faith in what God has said about you, in what he's shown you. If it hasn't happened yet, continue to walk in faith. Continue to serve others and tell them how great your

God is. God likes when we brag about him, there is nothing that is going on that he doesn't know about. You will see the word of God manifested in your life. Don't lose faith. I could have given up many times. The journey of a dreamer isn't easy and all sunshine and roses. I am here today writing this book to tell you that whatever God has said about you shall come to pass.

Through faith, whatever you do in the world will be amplified in Christ when you're in alignment. If you're a dreamer, keep dreaming. If you're a visionary, keep being a visionary. Hold on to the promises of God and the word of God, and place him in all that you do.

## *"If you want to go higher in life, go deeper in Christ." - LANGU*

The Creative ways God speaks to you and through you

# *LET'S UNPACK*

- ➤ What talents have you buried?
- ➤ Are you serving others?
- ➤ Is God Enough?

**Matthew 25:28- 29** So take the talent from him and give it to him who has the ten talents. For to everyone who has will more be given, and he will have an abundance. But from the one who has not, even what he has will be taken away

**Matthew 23:11-12** The greatest among you will be your servant. For those who exalt themselves will be humbled, and those who humble themselves will be exalted.

- Heavenly Father, In the name of Jesus Christ of Nazareth, reveal to me my talents, show me how to use them to glorify you, Take me deeper into your presence, hide me in your marvelous light so that others will be able to see you through me. Open my understanding and fill it with what I need to trust you more. Give me dreams, and visions, and strengthen me on the journey to fulfill my purpose.

# ESSENTIAL - LANGU

Say, Lord Speak to me and begin writing, or drawing by faith.

# Foresight

"Foresight" chapters will strengthen your faith; these chapters will speak to you and guide you as you venture into what God has for you. Using the word of God so that you can hear. Now, there is a prophetic anointing that flows into what foresight can be. So, if you have faith, this will increase your faith and make you more aware of what to look out for on your journey and how to maneuver. I want to add that this, however, does not replace the word of God, you should do your due diligence to study the word. This entire section will be taken from the book of Genesis, Chapters 39-45.

# Chapter 1

# FORESIGHT - COVID

## Covid - Foresight: Multicolored Dreamers

I want to dissect the life of Joseph. I believe that there will be many Josephs that will read this book. The story of Joseph can be found in the bible in the book of Genesis, chapter 37-50.

Joseph is a son, he's a brother, he's a family member. The book of Genesis chapter 37 starts off by telling you about a 17-year-old boy. Now, he would seem like a normal teenager, except there is something that is distinctively different about Joseph.

The thing about Joseph is that he has a blended family. Siblings, brothers, to be exact, that do not share the same mother, and we read early on that his brothers are not too fond of him.

The book of Genesis tells us about what Joseph does, he's shepherding, I'm sure, to him, he's just doing whatever is before him. Jacob, his father, loved him more than his other children. Joseph was the favorite. He loved him more, just enough that he gave him a different type of tunic. This tunic was multicolored. A tunic, a type of coat that people in this time would wear back in those times.

Now, I want to highlight that in life, there are some people who receive more favor than others. There are some people who have been gifted a multicolored tunic. We all know someone who has this kind of favor. Every family has a Joseph.

You might be asking yourself the question: Who is Joseph in my family? Well the answer isn't always so easy to digest.

After Joseph receives this gift, he is hated for it. His own brother grew more hatred towards him because of envy and jealousy. This meant he was no longer in an environment that was friendly. He was in a hostile environment.

Imagine being in a room with people you know don't like you. The reason why they don't like you isn't even something you did, but it was what you received.

Joseph is the person who is disliked in the home. He is the one who receives the dirty looks. He is the one who is isolated. He is the one who often plays by himself. Joseph is the one who is different, and everyone knows it. He might even look different from everyone else. Joseph is not just different, but people recognize that difference.

Joseph is the one who receives the dream. The thing about Joseph's character is that he can not recognize his difference amongst his brothers. This means that Joseph is vulnerable and open. He cares enough to share his dreams even when no one cares to hear them.

Joseph shared the dream he received, and his brothers hated him more. They hated him more because they presume that Joseph is being arrogant. They presume that Joseph is showing off. They secretly want to be like Joseph.

## *"It's okay to be different" - LANGU*

To whom much is given, much is also required. The dreamer with the multi-colored tunic is the person who is not only dreaming of big things but has a multifaceted skill set. It's the person who's not just multifaceted but also multi graced. This person just seems to always have the answer, or have the idea, and not only have the dream but have the favor to back it up.

What is required of such a person? This is why it's important to understand seasons in your life. Covid was a season that not only affected the world, but also, individually affected lives.

## *"Seasons are not random but ordained by God." - LANGU*

The foresight of Covid in my life taught me that with that gift of being the Joseph, with a multi-color tunic and a dreamer, will cause an intense level of frustration. Affecting not only you but anyone who is around you.

Covid exposed things in my life that needed to align with God's word and plan for my life. Before you come to Christ and even after, it's about trusting and knowing that God has a plan because he's the one who gave you the dream.

Life isn't just a random set of events. Everything in your life has a purpose. In my life, all the arguments brewing in this season pushed me to dream, create, write, and try to use my talents. What we miss is the foresight that God is using these real-life moments to build me up your ministry in the kingdom of God.

Even if it's something you don't have a thought about. Ministry was not a desire of mine. However, the pressures of my life caused me to revert into a mindset of reflection and introspection.

## *"They say art imitates life, in every person, there is a ministry. Something that God placed in you that doesn't just benefit you but it benefits others, and ultimately brings them closer to God." –*

### *LANGU*

With all that in mind, there are places we have to be at a certain point in time. We all are so precious to God, and he is so intentional about those who he has called and chosen. There are people who will have to hate us.

Personally speaking, prior to covid, I stepped away from creating. I stepped away from music to chase money. In my ideology, I thought that I was doing the right things. I was doing what everyone else was doing, especially with a baby in the mix, and knowing it comes with responsibilities.

I believe God used covid and the people around me to benefit me through priceless experiences. Even if those experiences seemed immensely frustrating and very uncomfortable.

Can you imagine that God loves you so much and is so intentional about you that even the seasons of trouble are a part of his design for your growth?

Let's take another look at Joseph from the bible. It wasn't God's plan for Joseph to stay around his family. Joseph's Garments were different. They were Multi-colored, Multi-dimensional.

Some of us have a different level of grace in our lives. Some are wearing different types of garments based on what God placed in them. It was God who gave Joseph a dream because he made him a dreamer.

There are many people whom God is giving a dream to. However, when God gives them the dream, he doesn't tell them how they are going to get there.

The journey is unknown. If many of us knew where we needed to be all the time, most of us wouldn't take the journey. Many of us would take the journey our own way.

The moment Joseph shared his dream with his family, it exposed parts of them that he didn't even know about. Your dream, what God gifted you with, will expose others around you. The sinful parts of others will manifest the moment you begin to share your dreams.

If I knew that sleeping around would cause soul ties I wouldn't have done it. If I understood that sleeping with someone would birth a season and period of my life that would propel me into depression, alcoholism, and regret, I certainly would have thought twice.

However, isn't it amazing that in the midst of a storm, I can be reminded of a dream, and that dream was to become a world-renowned artist and finally be free from my depression and reality.

Being creative is something that is therapeutic for me. Much like Joseph, I shared my dream with others. The biggest question is "WHY". Why was I so compelled to feel accepted by others? Why did I care enough to want to share?

If you follow the story of Joseph, you'll find that after he shared his dream with others, it caused a chain-reaction of events in his life. His own brothers plotted against him because of his dream.

## The Chain Reaction of Exposure

Your worst enemies are already around you, it's just that you haven't started to follow the dream that God gave you yet. His own flesh and blood would throw him down in a pit. When you enter into your dreaming season and vision season, understand what's coming with that.

When God gives you a dream, it comes with disruption. When God gives you a dream, it will disrupt your entire life. God gave him a dream, and it caused his entire life to be disrupted. If you're a dreamer or God has given you a vision, I want you to know that when you share that dream, it will cause disruption.

We do not always have the knowledge of what the journey is going to be like. Do not live in fear, but live in the truth of Jesus Christ. Even when you mean well, all of a sudden, things change on the drop of a dime. Find comfort in knowing who is with you. Sometimes, your enemies might turn out to be your relatives, and show love and compassion. People may plot to kill your dreams and plot various ways to bring you down. However, not even your enemies know the journey that God has you on, and remember, who is with you.

# Chapter 2

# FORESIGHT - NO STRESS

### No Stress - Foresight: Irritated and Striving

Did you know that there are some clams in the ocean that do not manufacture pearls. Only a select amount of clams will ever actually produce pearls. In fact, the process of making pearls isn't pleasant for the clams.

It all starts when a little piece of sand slips into the clam, causing the clam to become irritated. This irritation lasts for a season, a time, a moment. It's in this process of irritation that pearls are formed.

It's in these moments in our lives where it seems like everything is getting better, then out of nowhere, a close friend or family member will begin to hate you.

Then, eventually, things in your life will start falling apart. It's in these seasons of our lives when God gives us a vision or a dream.

It's in these moments that the devil fights you the hardest. It's in these moments that your current environment around you will never match the dream or the vision God gave you.

This can drive you insane trying to figure out how you're going to reach that dream or that vision. How are you going to reach the mountaintop heights when it seems like you're falling in the lowest valleys?

# "It's in the moments of irritation, that you can be confident you're getting ready to birth a pearl." - LANGU

God gives Joseph the dream, he gives him the vision. He shared this vision with his brothers and family. None of them received it well because the dream and vision meant that he would be elevated.

Most of the time, dreamers who carry that Joseph anointing dream bigger than where they currently are. Understand that when God gives you a dream, it's beyond what you can imagine. God did not only gave Joseph one dream, but he gave him 2.

There are those who will receive multiple visions, and multiple dreams. I want to speak to you directly. You are in place right now, questioning your ability. Questioning if you're dreaming too big. Can I declare in your life that you serve a very Big God. God likes to show off because everything he created is good, and then it's very good.

This second dream caused Joseph's brothers to secretly hate him even more and ultimately plot against him. There are people who will secretly plot against you. It's not your job to stop them.

We tend to focus our attention more on those who will try to stop us. We often talk more about that than we do about the dream giver, who is God. We should understand that no one can close a door God has opened.

Many times, there is a fear that we have of others, which is what stops our dreams. If God has given you a dream, declare that dream. Our fears to talk about our dreams and visions is what causes us not to live out our dreams. The Bible says the Lord is not a spirit of fear but power, love, and a sound-mind.

This is why sometimes God will not show us the journey.

The journey isn't always what we think. Joseph was sent to help his brothers by his father. Along the way, he became lost, so he asked for help.

There are people on your journey who will point you in the direction of destiny. Even Joseph became lost on his journey. When he became lost, he had to stop and ask for directions. It's important that we know what we are searching for. Joseph was sent with a dream and a multicolored covering.

Oftentimes, what we are looking for is not what we get when we find it. When we get that thing, it's not what we thought it would be. How many times, as a dreamer do we become lost? How many times along the way do we lose our way, and then we ask for directions?

Sometimes, what God sends you to look for isnt as it appears. It's a setup for the elevation. It's the fall for the rise. It's the downfall for the uprise. The Bible says that when Joseph finally found his brothers, they already saw him before he saw them.

Your downfall isn't random, but it's a plot. When others are planning your demise, keep on the path. Sometimes, God will let you know that you are being set up so that you understand that it will be for a testimony. So that you understand that it will be for a step up.

When his brothers saw him they decided to throw him down into a pit. It was originally the plan of the brothers to actually kill Joseph however, there was a brother that interceded on Joseph's behalf.

I can boldly declare that God gave me a different type of grace in life. The evidence is seen after returning from Jamaica. The thing is, even though I loved creating music, I had spent time trying to bury that talent. God allows things in my life to happen to push me on a journey. God would allow others to set me up so I can trust in him more.

Sometimes, God will give you a talent, a dream, or a vision, and then send you on a journey. When you start to follow that dream or vision it will feel like your whole life starts unraveling. Your own family will begin to remind you of where you're coming from. It's your own that will not be able to accept you.

I wrote the lyrics in the airport immediately after my trip to Jamaica. There's no way that I'd be able to write such a song that was believable if it wasn't for the fact that I was indeed stressed. In order for me to even begin to sing or create from that place, I had to own the greatness that was inside of me. I believe I had been shying away from trying to reach dreams because of the lack of support from my family.

When Joseph started to wear what his father gave him, it caused even more envy. The more he shared his dream with his family, the more they despised him. The person who is the dreamer is often only seen as arrogant, especially when talking about their dream or vision. It's because they take God at his word, and the faith that they have is God given. The fact that they can believe in something far beyond what they have seen or experienced isn't something to be taken lightly.

## *"The more you that you are, the more authentic that you are, the more people will dislike you." - LANGU*

There is nothing Joseph could have done to get his brothers to like him. Likewise, as a dreamer, there is nothing you can do to get people to like you. There is nothing you can do to get anyone to accept you. Some people were designed to be your opposition. Some people were designed to fight you. Some were designed to betray you. You cannot become consumed by who a person is supposed to be. Allow everyone to be who they are and trust in what people show you. Stay in the will and hands of God by obedience, and everything will turn out how it should.

## The Power of Location

The assignments that you'll have as a dreamer may seem obscure in relation to what God showed you. Sometimes, God places something in you, but that thing cannot be accomplished where you currently are. There is power in locations. There is destiny in location. Joseph had to venture into the pit. That was his destiny.

Considering what was to come in my life, considering where I am currently, where I was didn't seem to make sense at the time. I was following the lead of the holy spirit when I prayed before recording. Even though the song had nothing to do with God.

A Lot of the times, these moments serve as points that show us how much faith we have. No one knows the plans of God and how God will do things. The Bible says we should acknowledge God in all our ways, and he will direct our paths. There is power in prayer. It doesn't matter what you're doing once you acknowledge God, there is a release of directions for you. The thing is, oftentimes, we don't understand or see that it is God who is directing us, it is God who is sending us to a pit.

In what areas of your life are you neglecting to include God? Then how much are we limiting God? I'm not saying that we should, as a believer and follower of Jesus Christ, go and thoughtfully commit sin. When God gives you a dream, or a vision, the Journey may not be what you presume it to be. I want us to understand that the journey doesn't look the same for everyone.

Sometimes, religion and the will of God does not always align. Sometimes, a lot of fear and delay in the church is because of the spirit of religion. You must do your due diligence to walk your journey with confidence in who God has called you to be and what he has placed in you. This is not an excuse to sin because the bible teaches that we must live by the commands of God, no matter what.

## "TRUST GOD EVEN WHEN YOU

## LOSE TRUST IN OTHERS!" - LANGU

# Chapter 3

# FORESIGHT - CLUBHOUSE PROPHECY

## THE DREAMER

Now, not only was he thrown down into a pit, but he was now brought downward into slavery. Brought downward into Egypt. Now, in unfamiliar territory, unfamiliar regions, lands, and atmospheres. Joseph doesn't even understand what "Home" is.

Joseph doesn't even understand what the meaning of family is. However, no matter where the dreamer is, the dreamer is still wearing a multicolored coat. The dreamer still has that favor and covering.

The Dreamer is often mishandled for his dreams. The dreamer often becomes enslaved by family, friends, and even places. The dreamer never feels settled because the dreamer doesn't have a sense of home, or family. The dreamer is often robbed of the ability to feel because they have been in "survival mode."

## THE LESSON OF BETRAYAL

When we think of what practically happened to Joseph, we think about betrayal. Certain feelings are birthed from being betrayed. These feelings shape the person and mold the person's mind. It's like someone telling you fire is hot and can burn you versus touching fire and understanding it is hot and can burn you. The lesson that you learn or the wisdom you learn is how to 1. Identify fire, and 2. What happens after a fire burns you?

Dreamers often experience a lot of betrayal. The dreamer is often connected to the prophetic stream and has a strong sense of intuition. The reason for this is because of the lessons they learned from being burned. They are able to sense things others cannot. They also operate with the knowledge of how to move when they sense fire or danger.

Some things are hard to put into words, when the favor of God is on a person's life. Oftentimes, they may seem like nobody, they seem like nothing is going good for them, like nothing is going well with them.

Then, all of a sudden, they are elevated, and all of a sudden, they rise quickly; when they are involved in anything there is a strong influence and favor that they bring to the table that can only be described as supernatural, or some people understand the term favored.

The dreamer is often creative, and innovative; this is what creates opportunities for them. Their creative nature and their ability to think outside the box. The fact that they are dreamers gives them an edge and a different type of thinking pattern that isn't like others.

The plight of this is that it attracts power, jealousy, envy, and love, sometimes lust too. It's because this is a grace, it's a multicolored light. The dreamer of this caliber has to be very careful.

# SEARCHING FOR CONNECTION

Clubhouse was a platform where I expressed my creativity. Clubhouse was a platform that the Joseph in me, The boy who was searching for a home, was led to. Clubhouse filled the void in me of connection and purpose. However, Clubhouse trained me to listen. Clubhouse trained me how to give counsel, Clubhouse taught me how to take my issues and use them to help others by creating a space that isn't about stewing in your toxic traits but identifying them and healing from them.

Clubhouse was a glimpse of the power of vulnerability and influence. Even though I didn't realize it, it was the lord who was using me to connect and cause conversations to happen for deliverance. At the time, I wasn't thinking of it in this way. At the time, I wasn't fully submitted to God, which left room for error.

## THE EFFECT OF YOUR GIFTS

When Moses was sent to free God's people, Pharaoh came after him. When you use what God placed in you and it affects others and causes them to begin to become free, Pharaoh is coming after you. Now, Pharaoh, in this sense, is spiritual but affects the natural things around you.

After this global deliverance took place on Clubhouse, there was a wave of deliverance, and it affected not just my area or people I knew but others all over the world who I never met.

At the time, I just looked at it as a simple thing that happened by chance. Not understanding that it happened by divine influence. Not understanding it was a glimpse into my ministry and is the reason why I received my gifts. It's the reason for dreams and visions. It's not for you, but it's for your service to others.

This is where Pharaoh decided to show up by manipulating others. I was abandoned, left alone, and what I cared about the most was taken from me during a season that is all about family.

I felt isolated, I felt lonely. I felt robbed of my ability to show love. This was a common theme in my life. One minute, everything feels fine, but the next, I'm back in the pit of depression, the pit of loneliness, the pit of rejection, the pit of betrayal, the pit of confusion.

Pharaoh likes to strike when he thinks he has weakened your ability to feel. He likes to strike in moments when you return to the pit. So, although I was okay on the outside, I was escaping to a place where I could express how I was feeling. I wasn't equipped with the understanding. How to understand locations.

I now understand that the uneasy feeling in the studio was like a spiritual sense. The uneasy feeling was discernment in its infant nature. It's what happens when you aren't feeding your spirit, so your spirit is like a baby. Before a baby can verbally express words to you, it communicates through feelings. I was feeling something was off, I was feeling the fire, I was feeling the betrayal.

Innately, I understood that I had to move or else I would get burned. I couldn't see what was coming, I just knew "Run." I've felt this before, and I acted on this warning, this feeling, this intuition. I was lucky enough this time to see why I had to move. If I had left even 1 second later, we would be having a completely different conversation.

## Pray over the word

The thing about Clubhouse is that you can meet anyone there. The right people and sometimes the wrong people. I did not go there searching for a person; I went there looking for community. I have received prophetic words prior to this night. However, I did not know enough of the Word of God to properly discern and understand the word.

At the time, I was expecting to hear a rebuke. I was expecting to hear that I needed to get my life together and seek God's face like I had been told in the past. However, this was a different word. This word spoke more to what was currently going on in my life.

I was very skeptical at first and listened very keenly. Whenever I hear anyone mention "sewing a seed" I'm always very skeptical. The Bible warns us about "Wolves in sheep's clothing." Again, I was very young in the faith. I did not clearly understand who I was. I was a sinner living in sin. The word, however, gave me hope and increased my faith in God. It increased my faith in prayer and the prophetic. Was it a true word from "God"?

I believe that God can use anyone to speak into your life, and you can either accept the word or reject the word. At the time, I believed that it was God speaking through this servant. I didn't pray and ask God if it was true, but I prayed and asked for direction and protection.

Everything that he said was true based on what actually happened that very night before. Honestly, I went from no one knowing me, no one caring anything about what I was doing in life, I went from nothing to something that seemed like overnight.

Even in the midst of me living in sin, God still had his hand on me. Even though people wanted to kill me, God still kept his hand on me. Even though I was falling deeper into sin, God still kept his hand on me.

When God places something in you, satan wants to destroy you. He wants to destroy you because of what God will use you to do. He will try to get you to sin in front of God in order to mock God when he accuses you of falling into his traps and his devices. It's often Grace and Mercy that keeps us in these moments because God gave the gifts without repentance. Its favor that sustains us, and its a favor that we do not deserve.

*"A prophetic word is like a dream. It will cause people to hate you, it will cause warfare, people may even try to kill you."*

*- LANGU*

# Chapter 4

# FORESIGHT RUN

## There Is No Boundary To God's Blessing

Joseph is blessed, and Potipher knows it. Despite being in a place away from his home, it does not limit the reach of his blessing. God's blessings do not have limits. When God has a plan for your life, he will keep you. God promises us to never leave us or forsake us. When you're blessed, it's not just church people who can identify the blessing and favor that you carry.

Joseph is amongst Egyptians, unbelievers, sinners, and Idol worshippers. Joseph is in the land of Idolatry and false gods. Many times, dreamers will be amongst people who are not religious or even believers. Many times, the dreamers and visionaries will be in a place where they have no control. A place where the people in control can be considered "lost" or unbelievers.

## The Lesson of Dependency

Joseph had to fall downward into a pit in order to reach this place. When you find that you fall down and hit rock bottom, it humbles you. When you go from having, and begin to lose everything, it often teaches you to depend upon God for everything.

Your faith begins to flow from a place of desperation, Allowing you to operate with a different level of grace and humility because of the lessons of dependency.

Dreamers like Joseph usually have nothing or anyone else to depend on other than God. Near death experiences can teach many lessons. One of which is how fragile life really is outside the hands of God.

In addition, it can show you who is there for you in your times of need. Dreamer's often experience great lost's, long suffering, and heartbreak. They develop a dependence on God because they are forced to. They realize that everything can be taken away at any given moment.

## Uncommon Lands

All dreamers have the potential to be placed in positions of great influence and power; however, humility and humbleness is a necessity. This is a trait that must be taught.

Dreamers carry a different type of favor and grace because they have the ability and privilege to be in places that other believers are not graced to go.

Dreamers are often ridiculed for this and outcasted from the typical believers. Dreamers often have to walk the journey alone. This takes grace, wisdom, and understanding.

Joseph is a dreamer who has been graced to journey into an uncommon land. Despite his downward fall into his masters house, Joseph now has influence, power, and authority in the house of Potipher. Joseph receives this not because he is qualified, or the most talented, he receives this favor from Potipher because Potipher realizes that Joseph is special. He receives favor because Potipher perceived that God is prospering Joseph.

When the hand of God is on your life, even unbelievers will be able to see that grace and favor. Even unbelievers can benefit from someone with an anointing like Joseph.

*As a dreamer or visionary, you will attract many types of people. - LANGU*

God partners with man so that he can get the glory. Others can identify what God has placed in you despite you coming from nothing, others can identify what's transpiring in your life can only be an act of God.

## The Lessons of Humility & Humbleness

Some dreamers typically do not like to show off; they just care about completing the assignments to bring their vision to life. Some dreamers, however, receive elevation and end up falling because of pride.

There is a subtle power in humbleness and humility that God's chosen dreamers and visionaries will have to master. The reason dreamers have to master this in order to elevate is that Pride comes from Satan. Dreamers have access to the holy spirit through a righteous lifestyle.

The dreamer or visionary is often in a strange place. Similarly, like, Joseph. Potiphers wife wanted to sleep with Joseph because of what was on him. She wanted to attach herself to what was in him, which is the favor and the grace and the anointing. She wanted to defile Joseph. She wanted him to sin against God.

Most dreamers or visionaries will be tempted to knowingly "SIN" against God. The thing about strange lands is that there are also strange women. Women, meaning religions and practices. Don't lose yourself in the strange land, but remember your God. Many forces will try to defile dreamers and exploit them.

Joseph must remember what God has spoken over his life, and remember where God has brought him from. Even in his betrayed season, his slave season, his down season he must remember what God showed him.

## "Exercise Faith" - LANGU

When, where, and what you see currently does not match what God showed you, still believe. Run away from the things that you know within your heart are wrong. Run away from knowingly sinning against God. Run away from the people who want to use what God gave you against God.

## *"Use what God gave you for his glory."*

### *- LANGU*

## Dimensions of Reinvention

Dreamers or visionaries will have many temptations that, even when they resist them, they will still fall. It's important for the dreamer to understand that with every new level, there is a new devil. Passing a temptation doesn't mean you won't be tempted again. A new downward fall doesn't mean you failed the test.

Joseph is tempted and runs away. He runs away, but his coat is snatched off of him. Even though he is innocent, He is still accused because of how deceitful Potiphers wife is. The Bible says that the heart of man is deceitful and desperately wicked.

Dreamers often are in places amongst people who will betray them. Betrayal often comes from those around you. For dreamers and visionaries in strange lands. Wherever you are is an assignment. The first betrayal came from "Joseph's Brothers," and the second came from "Potiphers wife." These both came with a stripping of garments and what appears to be a "downward trajectory."

Downward into the pit caused Joseph to create a new identity. He had to reinvent himself, Upward, eventually, he reached Egypt and Potiphers house. Joseph reinventing himself didn't change his favor, grace, gifts, or blessings. It only caused him to learn more skills and gain wisdom.

## *"Embrace the downs, Reinvent yourself for each season of your life" -*

### *LANGU*

Oftentimes, opportunities to reinvent yourself come from situations that feel like a loss. Dreamers and visionaries experience a lot of these. However, they have learned to adapt to the ever changing uncertainty. Dreamers and visionaries have the ability to adapt to life's circumstances because they've been graced to go through it. Joseph is now sent down into the king's prison.

Dreamers and visionaries often are up against thrones because of what they are carrying. A throne represents power, and authority. The authority to control powers. This is why Joseph was thrown into the king's prison because of the level that Joseph was on. The king's prison is literally down below, it's literally rock bottom.

## *"They cannot kill you before your time, even in great suffering, Trust in GOD."*

### *- LANGU*

# Chapter 5

# FORESIGHT - FAVOR IN MY LOWEST

## Blessings in uncommon places

The king's prison is where the king sent his people who plotted against him. Potipher sent Joseph to a place where he would never see the light of day. Dreamers often will find themselves in captivity. The enemy of dreamers and visionaries often has plans to put them down or suck them dry. The forces that are against the dreamer and visionary are always seeking to finish the dreamer. The person with the vision is always put in places that are considered the low of lowest. This can be a physical place, or sometimes, the visionary is more often than not regarded and treated as the lowest person.

This alone can sometimes cause captivity physically, mentally, or emotionally. However, despite this, who God blesses, no man can curse. It doesn't matter where Joseph is, it doesn't matter what is stripped from Joseph. He still has the favor of the lord.

God shows him favor in the sight of the keeper of the prison. We often have an expectation that God will show up in our lives in a specific way, however, in most cases, that isn't always the way he'll show up. This means that there is a pattern of favor that is with Joseph. No matter where God grants him favor, it's always individuals who are in authority that recognize his God given favor. Oftentimes, the reason why we fail to prosper is because we block our destiny helpers, because we allow our environment to dictate who we connect with.

Dreamers usually prosper wherever they are; this isn't because of anything other than what God has placed in them. When God gives you a vision and graces you to accomplish something, he will provide provision. As a dreamer, it's important to know who you are.

## *"You can find God anywhere if you are looking for him." - LANGU*

If you're a dreamer or a visionary, It's time to stop blocking your own blessings based on our past fears and presumptions. Stop looking for people in where you are in life and start searching for God. That will reveal to you the people you are meant to connect with.

### Down with Authority

Joseph, The dreamer, The visionary, is down but not out. Joseph is elevated in prison because God is with him. When God places something in you, when you are called to be a leader, you will walk in that calling. Joseph was destined to become a leader, someone with authority. Most dreamers often get discouraged in life because of where the vision takes them. The vision God gives you might take you into circumstances of high stress. The vision might come with many disappointments.

Even in those moments, remember that God is with you. When you find yourself as a dreamer in a position that you didn't intend nor did you desire, then remain there until God opens a door for you. Many times, we are in undesirable situations, and we check out before we complete our assignment.

Sometimes, we begin to do our own thing and forget who we are. Sometimes, we forget what God has placed in us.

## *"Don't neglect your gifts and talents*

*even when you're not in the position you think you should be in." - LANGU*

Whatever Joseph did, the bible says the lord made it prosper. For dreamers, it's important to be where God wants you to be, so that you can prosper. Your prosperity comes because God is with you. When God gives you that dream or that vision, hold on to it. Everything you'll need in life is tied to the vision that is in you. Do not go against what God placed in you. If you're a dreamer, then keep on dreaming, if your gift is writing, then keep on writing, if your gift is preaching, then keep on preaching. Whatever vision he gives you, work at it relentlessly with great faith.

## *"Don't intend to use your gifts to obtain money, or relationships, or power. Use your gifts to serve others." - LANGU*

In his prison season, Joseph meets two individuals. They are described as being "The Butler" and "The Baker".

### The Right Connection

Every season has a purpose, and every season has people for you to meet. Joseph connects with these two individuals in prison. Never underestimate the people around you. Sometimes, great people, influential people, and geniuses find themselves on their way down. Some people who are in these situations are coming from places you desire to be. Sometimes, people who are in their "down" season are only passing by to launch into the higher heights of their lives at the time of "UP."

Joseph could have allowed where he was to change his attitude towards others. Instead, Joseph allowed the Christ in him to be seen. He wasn't only thinking about himself even in the season of his life where he is confined to a prison. Even in the season of his life where he was in another pit, even in the season of his life where he has nothing. He was still in a frame of mind of helping others.

As a dreamer, it's important to understand that you are a servant. It doesn't matter what season you are in, you are called to serve. Remember that elevation comes with understanding that there are others who are counting on you. The same people you see now can experience elevation tomorrow. They can be the same ones that pull you to higher dimensions.

Joseph ministers to these two individuals. Using the gift that God gave him. It is never mentioned in the Bible that Joseph can interpret dreams. However, Joseph understands that interpretations come from God. Now, this has a double meaning.

Your dreams can only be understood by connecting to God, who is the source of interpretations. Many times, we need directions in life so that we can fulfill our purpose. As a dreamer or visionary, seek God for answers. This is the cause for some dreamers and visionaries to die before their time.

It has been said that the cemetery is one of the richest places on earth because many people die with their greatness and die with their dreams and visions.

Dreamers and visionaries must never lose faith and their connection to God. It was by faith that Joseph was able to interpret the dreams. It was by faith and favor that God allowed whatever Joseph spoke out of his mouth to come to pass.

As dreamers and visionaries chosen by God, we must be mindful of what we say and how we interpret life. We must steward over the gift of interpreting life and use it to glorify God. Dreamers are often wise beyond their years. This is because of the connection they have with God. It must be used to serve others with pure intentions according to the leading of the holy spirit. If you're a dreamer but lack the belief in God or find that you are struggling in that area, it's vital to strengthen that.

## *"Don't underestimate your trust in God"* - *LANGU*

Do not become upset when people forget how you helped them. Oftentimes, as a dreamer, you will be used by many people. You have to become ok with being a servant and never receiving credit.

## *"All the glory belongs to Jesus."* – *LANGU*

All that you have is given to by God, his timetable is different from our timetable. The Bible says faith without works is dead. It's important to continue to work even when you do not receive credit. It's important to know that your source of happiness and validity does not lie with man, but it's in God. It's important to learn the lesson of who's word to trust. Once you master trusting God's word above all else, you will experience real peace even in extreme conditions.

## *"Rely on God and God alone, when things don't go how you expected them to, it's because God has a bigger and better plan."* - *LANGU*

# Chapter 6

# FORESIGHT JUST IN TIME

It doesn't matter how much time goes by God will allow you to receive what he has for you. Joseph was in prison for two full years after the chief butler and baker came out of prison.

As a dreamer, you cannot compare yourselves to others. Sometimes, you will be in situations longer than others, you might struggle harder and longer, and greater. Sometimes, as a dreamer or a visionary, you will be down for a longer period of time.

As a dreamer, it might seem like you're being stretched thin, sometimes, it might seem like God has forgotten about you. Seeming like God is pulling you downward and keeping you there.

## Potential & Kinetic Energy

In physics, there are two different types of energy I want to highlight. One is potential energy, and the other is kinetic energy. Now, potential energy is also referred to as stored energy. The power of stored energy is the moment in time that it is released. That energy now converts to kinetic energy, which refers to motion.

Your season of stretching is a downward stretch pointed in a designated direction based on the word. God is allowing all your potential to be stored up during your stretching. There

83

will be a moment in time when you will be launched.

The direction is based on the word because the word is your aiming and carrying system. The potential that has been stored up for all those years will launch you to higher heights, the word will carry you further than those you have seen come and go.

## *"Embrace your season of stretching because your launch is inevitable." - LANGU*

The bible says that Pharaoh had a dream, and by design, no one in his immediate reach could interpret his dream. This tells the dreamer that, when it's the appointed time to fulfill your destiny, no one will be able to steal it from you.

There are things, places, and moments, that your name and your name only is written on. As a dreamer, your name will often enter rooms that your feet have not yet been in. Your name will be brought up amongst greatness because greatness is in you already, it will be in rooms with leaders and influencers because that is already in you.

As a dreamer or visionary, you do not have to worry about missing what God has for you. What God has for you is attracted to what God spoke about you and placed in you.

## *"You cannot miss what has been predestined for you." - LANGU*

So Joseph is called up from the down season, up from that low place. Subsequently, the dreamer Joseph is cleaned up, with the prison being shaved from him. Joseph is transformed, with new garments being placed on him.

As a dreamer, you must understand that you have the ability to adapt to changing environments. This means that wherever you find yourself, you must embrace it. Don't try to be where you're coming from, but grow with where you go.

You cannot bring a prison mentality to the palace and vice versa. Every new season of your life you'll have to shave off the former things to embrace the new. New look, new clothes, new people, new ideas, new strategies. The only thing that remains the same is God.

It doesn't matter how down and out you were, what is in you is greater than your current environment. In like the blink of an eye, Joseph was standing before Pharaoh. As a dreamer, you have to live everyday like you're ready for anything to take place in your life. You cannot allow frustration to overtake you. You cannot allow the moment of pits and prisons to shrink you.

## *"You were caught in a small pond, but don't stop swimming because you're about to be released in a big ocean." - LANGU*

Just like Josspeh, your life can change in the blink of an eye. All your dreams can come true overnight, are you ready? Joseph was now entering a new season; he was brought to Pharaoh. It doesn't matter how long it took; his position was always waiting for him.

When Pharaoh asks Joseph to interpret his dreams, Joseph does one key thing that every dreamer and visionary must learn, adopt, and practice. The Bible says, "So Joseph answered Pharaoh, saying, 'It is not in me' God will give Pharaoh an answer of peace." In other words, Joseph is boldly proclaiming that there is nothing special about him whatever he does comes from God.

## *"It's GOD WILL"- LANGU*

Joseph reached a place of knowing and being dependent on God. Reaching this place as a dreamer takes pit experiences, it takes trials and tribulations. Reaching this place takes knowing that you're not in control and whatever happens is not your will but God's will.

This causes Joseph to show up and give God glory. Joseph could not have arrived at this place mentally, or spiritually unless he was coming from a down season. Joseph is elevated to second in command in all of Egypt. This comes with more blessings than he has ever anticipated. Joseph is experiencing soaring in spheres that require wisdom and humbleness.

The time he spent in the down season was building up potential energy. When it was finally released at the appointed time, it catapulted him into a sphere he never imagined. Sometimes, it's tough to hold on to your dreams, passions, and visions in seasons of down, but don't grow weary in serving.

## *"Have you submitted your will to God?" - LANGU*

Sometimes, the dreams and visions that God has given us require destiny helpers, and sometimes, God gives you wisdom and strategies to help others. However, oftentimes, we are so narrow sighted and focused on ourselves that we miss serving others. We use what God gave us to only serve ourselves.

## *"Never miss an opportunity to serve"- LANGU*

There is a great lesson and blessing in serving. Do not hold onto others, do not try to pull anyone down, let it be your mission to be a blessing to others. This is what it means to operate with love, in love, and be about love.

Do not get caught up in self-gain that you refuse to release onto others. With a promise that God gave to Abraham, saying I will bless those who bless you. It is God's will that others will bless you, but you have to be a blessing also.

# Chapter 7

# FORESIGHT THE DREAM LINE

Joseph, The one who received the dream. Had to journey down a line that was unpredictable. The dream line is the journey. Joseph is in a position now of authority power, and influence. He is in a different season of life. Even in this season, it doesn't mean he gets to kick his feet up. He still has to work. A false ideology is thinking that once you are elevated, you'll get to rest from working. In fact, this is where there is real pressure, real stress.

To whom much is given, much is required. Joseph's life is on the line. What Joseph learned early on through trials and tribulations was to trust in God's word. As the dreamer, you'll be used to producing the solution to others' problems. Joseph received the strategy to help Pharaoh, and Pharaoh put him in charge of seeing it through.

## SEE IT THROUGH

It's easy to become complacent when you feel like you've gone through hell and back to be where you are. What is the secret to not becoming complacent? Well, as a dreamer, you should expect balance in your life. Rain brings sun. Dreamers will experience years of abundance. Dreamers will experience years of things being in excess. The dreamer needs to learn how to apply wisdom. The application of wisdom for a dreamer is important for the sustainability and longevity of a dreamer.

"SAVE!". It's smart for a dreamer to put something to the side when in a season of abundance. A dreamer must have the understanding that things can change on the drop of a dime. This takes great discipline. What the dreamer is actually doing is putting themselves and others in a position to survive the down season. Down seasons are inevitable! "Save for a rainy day" is a popular idiom that has biblical foundations. Joseph finds that in every season, there is work to be done.

Dreamers should understand that in every season of down or up, you must still rely on God. God can make you forget all your troubles and allow you to be fruitful in suffering. As a dreamer, you must understand that in the very place you felt like you were stuck, God can bless you. In the places you were once suffering, God can allow you to be fruitful. Dreamers understand that suffering produces great faith. This is why you must increase your faith. God can bless you anywhere.

God doesn't just use Joseph to bless Egypt, but he uses Joseph to bless the world. When the problem struck the world, it was Joseph who had the answer. The Pharaoh sent everyone to Joseph. Joseph was once just a nobody, he was once a slave, he was once a prisoner. Now, the entire world knew Joseph.

When God gives you a dream, believe in it. When God gives you a strategy, follow it. It's important for the dreamer not to lean on his understanding and towards his desires. Dreamers need wisdom from God to receive instructions from God and not from man. Literally, Joseph's obedience is what prepared him for the next season of Down.

## THE STOREHOUSE OF A DREAMER

His storehouse was the storehouse that was going to supply the world. The dreamline has its suffering, take confidence in knowing that the greater you suffer, the greater impact you'll have. Embrace your suffering season so that you can enjoy the seasons of abundance. The key thing to take away is the fact that Joseph was not a bitter man. Oftentimes, when some dreamers had to suffer, they become greedy, bitter, and mean.

Understandably, it's difficult to maintain an attitude of positivity. Find solace in gratitude! When you truly reach that mindset that everything is gifted to you from God, you become positive in the face of all opposition and situations.

Joseph is now put to the ultimate test. This test is the test to see if he still had love in his heart. Remember, those who betray you will still need you. Vengeance belongs to God.

Joseph's brothers ended up being the ones in front of him needing grain. At this moment, Joseph remembers the dream that God gave him. Joseph remembers the promises of God. Even though Joseph recognizes them, they do not recognize him.

Dreamers and visionaries often change beyond what anyone expects. Dreamers should not promote their successes or failures. This gives glory to God because those who counted you out will know that it had to be God. They say you never hear a tree growing. The dream that God gave you will shape you into who you were meant to be. Allow others to be shocked. Allow God to tell your story. God is a master revealer; he knows the right time to showcase you.

When God allows your dream to come true, how will you act? Your actions speak to who you are. Even though Joseph puts them all in prison and test's their honesty. During him testing their honesty, he told them that he feared God. As a dreamer with influence and power, the fear of God is the best way to make decisions. When you fear God, your actions are done with him in mind.

As a dreamer, you need honest people around you. You have to give others the chance, to be honest. Honesty is the best policy. Joseph decides to use one brother as a way to get the other brothers to return to Egypt. Despite his blessings, Joseph is still dealing with his real emotions. It's important to never let your emotions supersede what God wants. The fear of God must never leave you. As a leader, you must place your emotions to the side. Joseph weeps in private. It's okay to cry, it's okay to feel what you've been through. You don't have to become like a robot. The dream line requires that you walk in the spirit while being in the flesh.

## *"Don't forget to feel"- LANGU*

God doesn't want us to ignore ourselves; he wants us to be aware of ourselves. Be present, be aware of how you're feeling, and be honest about that. This gives you control over your emotions and not the other way around. As dreamers and visionaries, don't neglect your emotional intelligence. Even if you need to take a minute to express yourself.

Joseph still loves his family. Love is something that all of us feel. We are made to love. Dreamers will find themselves having great compassion for others. The reason why dreamers have so much compassion is that they have been tested greatly. Once you've been broken down and depend on God, it is impossible to connect with God and not have compassion for others. To know God is to know love.

Joseph now makes a plan to reconnect his family, reconnect with his father and brothers. A fathers love is important for dreamers. A father is the one who instills courage and confidence in dreamers. Fathers are important to dreamers. Fathers serve as the first human beings to encourage us on where to go. It was his father who gave him his coat of many colors. Fathers are an earthly extension of our heavenly fathers.

Dreamers never forget who believed in them. Joseph wants to make his father proud. God is intentional about those he chooses. God knows the heart and intentions, he created the dreamer with a purpose.

Joseph's brothers come back to Egypt, they are washed and treated with kindness. They get to sit at the table with Joseph. Dreamers and visionaries will often eat at the table with enemies. However, the hand of God is in your life. No one can kill who God has said should live. This day was prepared before they even arrived in Egypt.

It's this reason dreamers shouldn't worry about enemies or haters. Dreamers should focus on serving and showing up in all seasons, confident and cheerful. Dreamers should never be afraid. In your" up" seasons or "down" seasons, continue to show love, and serve others. Continue to shine. A dreamer should never dim his or her light. Use your light to show others the way.

Joseph is serving his enemies, who just happen to be his brothers. Never stoop low, even when you have the opportunity, too. The dream line isn't all about suffering, it's also about forgiveness and serving. You'll have to dig deep in order to do this.

The opportunity to tell his brothers the truth arises, but Joseph chooses to bring them to a point of all honesty. Sometimes, as a dreamer, even though you want to bless others, you must wait until they are honest with you.

## *"Sew into honesty!"* - *LANGU*

Don't settle for dishonesty. When you recognize that there are honest people around you, that is when you know it is the right time. When they finally tell Joseph the truth, he decides to reveal who he is. It's not your job to reveal who you are until the right time presents itself. If people don't know who you are, that is okay. It's not every environment that you need to announce who you are.

As a dreamer, you belong to God. Allow God to place you in the position before you move. The line of a dreamer is the line of ultimate reliance in God. Dreamers go before others in their family so that God can save lives. Joseph understands this because of his connection to God.

Dreamers need to stay connected to God. Everything that happened in Joseph's life was designed by God. The dreamer's journey is predestined. Dreamers are usually in a deliverance ministry. Dreamers deliver families out of struggles, out of poverty, and lack. Dreamers open doors for their family. The Dream is designed to teach how to be more Christ- like.

Dreamers are the people God uses to raise up families. Dreamers are oftentimes the black sheep. Don't allow anyone to kill your dreams, don't allow anyone to stop you from helping your family. Keep dreaming, keep being a visionary. Sometimes, the only way up is the way down.

# INSIGHT

"Insight" chapters will give brief summaries of each chapter's themes. Delving into the importance of mental health and extrapolating therapeutic techniques from each theme. You can choose to implement some of these practices.

# Chapter 1

# INSIGHT - COVID

Chapter 1: Insight, Covid

## Theme 1: Overwhelmed by Life's Demands

In the wake of the COVID-19 pandemic, the protagonist finds themselves juggling college, a demanding school system job, and part-time work at a hospital. Despite financial stability, they're emotionally and mentally drained, struggling to balance the pressures of work and family life. Their home environment becomes toxic, further compounding their stress. The chapter explores themes of burnout, isolation, and the early cracks in their mental health.

*Psychological Insight:*

The protagonist's experience highlights the debilitating effects of burnout, which can lead to feelings of inadequacy and a sense of drowning even when surrounded by others.

*Therapeutic Techniques:*

- **Cognitive-Behavioral Therapy (CBT):** Reframe negative thoughts about self-worth to foster resilience.

- **Mindfulness Practices:** Use breathing exercises or meditation to anchor themselves during moments of overwhelm.

- **Journaling:** Write reflections to better understand triggers and emotions.

---

## Theme 2: Escaping Through Substances

As the pressures mount, the protagonist turns to alcohol and weed as coping mechanisms. What begins as occasional use escalates into dependency, becoming a way to numb emotional pain. Their days blur into a cycle of smoking and drinking, and their once vibrant personality becomes a shadow of itself. Despite this, they continue functioning—working, and trying to maintain appearances, but inwardly, they're unraveling.

*Psychological Insight:*

Substance use often arises as a method of self-soothing in the absence of healthier coping strategies. This dependency signals unaddressed emotional distress.

*Therapeutic Techniques:*

- **Motivational Interviewing (MI):** Explore the benefits of sobriety and identify internal motivations for change.

- **Harm Reduction:** Gradually reduce consumption while adopting healthier outlets, like physical exercise or creative pursuits.

- **Group Therapy:** Build a support network through peer groups like AA or NA.

---

## Theme 3: Creativity as Solace

Amid the chaos, the protagonist rediscovers their passion for music. Spending time with artists and producers, they find a sense of belonging and validation through creativity. Their cousin's home studio becomes a haven where they can express themselves and learn about their family's artistic legacy. Music transforms from a hobby into a therapeutic outlet, helping them process emotions and escape the weight of their struggles.

*Psychological Insight:*

Creative expression serves as a powerful tool for emotional regulation, allowing the protagonist to channel their pain into art and reconnect with their identity.

*Therapeutic Techniques:*

- **Art Therapy:** Use songwriting and music production to explore and process emotions.

- **Flow Activities:** Engage in immersive creative sessions that foster a sense of peace and accomplishment.

- **Narrative Therapy:** Frame their story through music and lyrics, reframing struggles as sources of strength.

---

### Theme 4: Confidence Through Challenges

A transformative trip to Jamaica introduces the protagonist to a world of opportunities. Meeting established and emerging artists, they begin to see themselves as capable of navigating professional spaces. The experience of recording with notable producers and mingling with industry icons normalizes success, replacing idolization with respect and camaraderie. By the end of the trip, they've gained a newfound sense of self-assurance.

*Psychological Insight:*

Confidence often grows when individuals face challenges that push them outside their comfort zone. The protagonist's willingness to engage in new experiences fosters resilience.

*Therapeutic Techniques:*

- **Positive Psychology Exercises:** Reflect on accomplishments and recognize their unique talents.

- **Visualization of Success:** Envision thriving in spaces where their creativity is valued.

- **Goal-Setting:** Break larger aspirations into manageable steps to maintain momentum.

---

## Theme 5: Lessons from Nature and Energy

The chapter culminates with a profound moment of reflection atop Tony Rebel's studio. Observing a mango tree leaning toward the studio's positive energy becomes a metaphor for growth and alignment. The protagonist realizes the importance of surrounding themselves with environments that nurture their well-being and creativity. This lesson provides a guiding principle for their future.

*Psychological Insight:*

The mango tree's inclination toward positive energy symbolizes the human tendency to thrive in nurturing environments. This insight reinforces the value of intentional choices in relationships, routines, and surroundings.

*Therapeutic Techniques:*

- **Environmental Audits:** Regularly assess whether their environment supports their goals and mental health.

- **Gratitude Practices:** Acknowledge the sources of positivity in their life.

- **Energy Visualization:** Imagine themselves as a tree leaning toward the light, growing stronger and more resilient each day.

# Chapter 2

# INSIGHT - NO STRESS

The chapter begins with the protagonist returning from Jamaica, ignited by a creative spark and a newfound sense of clarity. Sitting in an airport terminal, he immerses himself in music, finding solace in creating lyrics that serve as affirmations: "You ain't gotta stress, baby." Despite his challenging circumstances—strained relationships, separation from his daughter, and the emotional toll of depression—he begins to use music as a therapeutic outlet.

This chapter explores the protagonist's journey through pain and self-discovery, anchored by five key themes:

---

### 1. The Therapeutic Power of Creation

**Psychological Insight:** Creativity serves as a natural form of therapy, engaging the brain's reward systems and promoting emotional regulation. Activities like songwriting allow individuals to externalize their inner turmoil, fostering a sense of control and relief.

**Integration in the Chapter:** Music becomes the protagonist's sanctuary. His improvisation at the airport marks the beginning of a transformative process, using melodies and lyrics to process his emotions. The repetitive affirmation in his lyrics, "You ain't gotta stress," acts as a self-soothing mantra, reaffirming his resilience.

**Therapeutic Technique:**

- **Journaling Through Art:** Encourage self-expression through creative outlets like writing, painting, or music to process emotions in a non-verbal way.

- **Affirmations:** Incorporating positive affirmations into creative work can reframe negative self-talk and foster a hopeful mindset.

---

## 2. Recognizing and Responding to Intuition

**Psychological Insight:** Intuition often serves as a psychological alarm system, signaling when something feels off based on past experiences and subconscious processing. Honoring intuitive feelings can be crucial for self-preservation.

**Integration in the Chapter:** The protagonist listens to his inner voice during two key moments: leaving a party early in Jamaica and refusing to speak with a dubious figure at a gathering. These instances highlight his growing self-awareness and ability to protect his boundaries.

**Therapeutic Technique:**

- **Mindfulness Practices:** Regular mindfulness exercises help enhance awareness of bodily sensations and emotional cues, strengthening intuitive decision-making.

- **Boundary Setting:** Learning to assertively say "no" when something feels wrong is a cornerstone of healthy emotional boundaries.

---

## 3. Resilience Through Spiritual Connection

**Psychological Insight:** Spiritual practices like prayer and meditation can promote resilience by reducing stress, providing a sense of purpose, and reinforcing self-efficacy.

Integration in the Chapter: Before recording his first song in the studio, the protagonist turns to prayer, seeking guidance and strength. This moment solidifies his commitment to aligning his artistic journey with a higher purpose, using his talents as a testament to his faith.

**Therapeutic Technique:**

- **Gratitude Journaling:** Reflecting on moments of spiritual or personal growth can enhance emotional resilience and foster a sense of purpose.

- **Guided Prayer or Meditation:** Incorporating structured spiritual practices can provide a grounding framework during periods of uncertainty or anxiety.

---

### 4. Navigating Recognition and Jealousy

**Psychological Insight:** Rising success often triggers interpersonal challenges, as others project their insecurities or envy onto the individual achieving recognition. Managing these dynamics requires emotional intelligence and self-regulation.

**Integration in the Chapter:** As the protagonist gains recognition for his music, jealousy surfaces among his peers. A vivid dream symbolizes these tensions, warning him of potential betrayals and the need to remain vigilant. His ability to process these challenges without succumbing to negativity showcases his growing emotional maturity.

**Therapeutic Technique:**

- **Cognitive Restructuring:** Practice reframing negative feedback or envy from others as a reflection of their struggles rather than a personal attack.

- **Social Support Systems:** Cultivate relationships with individuals who provide encouragement and constructive feedback.

---

## 5. Dream Analysis and Symbolism

**Psychological Insight:** Dreams often serve as a mirror to the subconscious, offering insights into unresolved conflicts, fears, and desires. Engaging with dream symbolism can illuminate hidden aspects of one's psyche.

**Integration in the Chapter:** The protagonist dreams of navigating a perilous warehouse filled with temptations and threats. The imagery—golden shirts, poisoned soup, and a climb to a studio at the pinnacle—represents his internal and external battles. This dream reinforces his determination to overcome challenges and remain focused on his goals.

**Therapeutic Technique:**

- **Dream Journaling:** Keeping a journal of dreams can help uncover recurring themes and patterns, fostering self-awareness.

- **Symbolic Exploration:** Reflect on dream imagery through writing or discussion to interpret its meaning in the context of current life challenges.

---

### Final Reflection

The protagonist's journey in this chapter demonstrates the transformative power of creativity, intuition, faith, and perseverance. Through music and prayer, he channels his pain into purpose, navigating personal and professional growth with grace. The challenges of success, jealousy, and spiritual testing only strengthen his resolve to remain true to his calling.

---

### Key Takeaways for Readers

1. **Art as a Healing Tool:** Engage in creative activities to process emotions and foster resilience.

2. **Trust Your Instincts:** Listen to your inner voice to navigate complex situations with clarity and confidence.

3. **Anchor Yourself in Faith:** Spiritual practices like reading the word of God can provide strength and purpose during times of adversity.

4. **Manage Interpersonal Dynamics:** Success requires maintaining boundaries and responding to conflict with emotional intelligence.

5. **Explore Your Subconscious:** Dreams can offer valuable insights into unresolved emotions and internal conflicts.

# Chapter 3

# INSIGHT CLUBHOUSE PROPHECY

## Chapter Summary

In this chapter, the narrative delves into the transformative power of faith, community, and intuition while exploring the protagonist's personal and professional growth. This period highlights the interplay between external challenges and internal spiritual guidance, weaving through moments of uncertainty, divine intervention, and self-reflection.

---

### 1. Faith and Divine Guidance

The protagonist finds themselves increasingly drawn to moments of spiritual intervention. From the uneasy feeling at the studio that prompts their departure to the prophetic encounter on the Clubhouse app, their faith becomes a compass. The prophetic word acts as a reminder of their purpose, rekindling their belief in their divine calling.

### Psychological Insight:

Faith often serves as a psychological anchor during periods of uncertainty. It offers a sense of control and purpose when external circumstances seem chaotic.

**Therapeutic Technique:**

- **Journaling Spiritual Encounters:** Writing down significant spiritual moments can help solidify their meaning and provide clarity for future decision-making.

- **Guided Visualization:** Envisioning the promises of faith fulfilled can enhance motivation and focus.

---

## 2. Community and Connection

The protagonist's time on the Clubhouse app fosters connections with diverse individuals across industries. The "My Toxic Traits" trend they initiate evolves into a support system where people share vulnerabilities. Despite feeling isolated during the holidays, this virtual community provides a sense of belonging and purpose.

**Psychological Insight:**

Shared experiences and communal support can mitigate feelings of isolation and loneliness, fostering resilience through human connection.

**Therapeutic Technique:**

- **Group Therapy Models:** Engaging in group discussions around shared themes, such as healing or overcoming challenges, mirrors the cathartic effect of the Clubhouse sessions.

- **Affirmation Exercises:** Encouraging others and receiving positive reinforcement can build a sense of mutual empowerment.

---

## 3. Intuition and Inner Wisdom

The protagonist repeatedly experiences intuitive "feelings," such as the urge to leave the studio on New Year's Eve. These moments signal their heightened self-awareness and connection to inner wisdom. This intuition ultimately helps them navigate dangerous and uncertain situations.

**Psychological Insight:**

Intuition is the subconscious processing of information. It often reflects lived experiences and an innate ability to recognize patterns or threats.

**Therapeutic Technique:**

- **Mindfulness Training:** Enhancing present-moment awareness can sharpen intuitive abilities.

- **Body Scanning:** Regularly checking in with physical sensations can help discern emotional or intuitive signals.

---

### 4. Self-Reflection and Personal Growth

The prophetic word acts as a catalyst for the protagonist to revisit past promises and dreams, reigniting their commitment to their creative and spiritual journey. Their recollection of being told they were special as a child ties to a recurring theme of feeling chosen for a higher purpose.

**Psychological Insight:**

Reflection on past affirmations and prophecies can reinforce self-concept and instill a sense of mission, especially during periods of doubt.

**Therapeutic Technique:**

- **Inner Child Work:** Reconnecting with the beliefs and affirmations instilled in childhood can restore a sense of wonder and purpose.

- **Cognitive Restructuring:** Challenging negative beliefs about their worth or capabilities in light of affirmations received.

---

### 5. Vulnerability and Transparency

The protagonist opens up to their manager about the prophetic word and their deep relationship with God. This transparency marks a turning point, allowing them to move forward with greater intention and discernment.

### Psychological Insight:

Authentic self-expression builds trust and strengthens relationships. It also provides relief from the burden of hiding significant parts of oneself.

### Therapeutic Technique:

- **Narrative Therapy:** Sharing one's story fosters empowerment and a deeper understanding of personal identity.

- **Boundaries Setting:** Ensuring that vulnerability is shared in safe spaces to maintain emotional security.

---

### Key Takeaways

1. **Faith as Strength:** The protagonist's belief in divine guidance shapes their decisions and fortifies their resilience.

2. **Community Healing:** Connections through the Clubhouse app highlight the power of shared experiences.

3. **Trusting Intuition:** Following their instincts leads to life-saving decisions and deeper self-awareness.

4. **Embracing Vulnerability:** Transparency about their spiritual journey deepens their commitment to their purpose.

### Closing Reflection

This chapter illustrates how faith, intuition, and community can transform isolation into empowerment. Through spiritual encounters, shared experiences, and introspection, the protagonist navigates their path with renewed purpose and clarity.

# Chapter 4

# INSIGHT - RUN

**Themes and Psychological Insights:**

### 1. Identity and Persona:

The chapter delves into the protagonist's struggle with maintaining a false persona, "TheTonyTyme," to mask deeper pain and insecurities. The facade of success contrasts sharply with the internal battle of self-worth and authenticity. This reflects the psychological theory of identity crisis, where the gap between the "real self" and "ideal self" creates dissonance.

### 2. Escapism and Coping Mechanisms:

Through drinking, smoking, and constant traveling, the protagonist seeks to escape from emotional pain, a common coping strategy for unresolved trauma. However, these temporary distractions compound the feelings of isolation and dissatisfaction. The chapter highlights the dangers of avoiding emotional healing by numbing oneself.

### 3. Faith and Prophecy as Anchors:

Faith emerges as a guiding force despite the chaos. The prophetic words serve as a beacon of hope, reaffirming the protagonist's purpose and providing a sense of direction amid turmoil. This aligns with the therapeutic concept of meaning-making, where individuals find purpose through spirituality or personal belief systems.

### 4. Trust and Vulnerability:

A recurring theme is the fear of intimacy and trust, born from past betrayals and disappointments. This fear manifests in behaviors like pretending to be high to eavesdrop on others and the inability to fully open up to those around him. The chapter explores how vulnerability can be both a source of connection and anxiety.

107

## 5. The Weight of Favor:

The idea of "favor" and its accompanying responsibilities illustrates the psychological burden of success. The protagonist grapples with imposter syndrome, questioning whether they deserve the opportunities they've received while sensing envy and resentment from others.

---

### Chapter Highlights:

- **Living Fast, Losing Control:**

The protagonist is caught in a whirlwind of hedonism, using substances and a party lifestyle to mask emotional pain. This lifestyle reflects a deep unhappiness stemming from missing his children and unresolved childhood trauma.

- **Running to Escape Reality:**

A pivotal moment occurs when he abruptly leaves for Atlanta on Thanksgiving morning, symbolizing his need to escape mounting pressures. This act of running mirrors a psychological flight response, where individuals flee perceived threats instead of confronting them.

- **Support and Pride:**

The kindness of a friend who provides financial assistance begins to challenge the protagonist's pride. This support underscores the importance of human connection and the role of humility in personal growth.

- **Atlanta and Renewed Hope:**

Despite personal struggles, the protagonist finds validation and encouragement in Atlanta. Encounters with industry professionals affirm his talent, while conversations with friends allow for moments of vulnerability and reflection. However, the weight of his struggles lingers, creating an internal conflict between hope and fear.

- **Spiritual Guidance:**

Prophetic words and advice from Maureen provide caution and direction, emphasizing the need for discernment and reliance on faith. These moments reaffirm the protagonist's belief in divine guidance, but also highlight his reluctance to fully embrace it.

- **Fear of Connection:**

The chapter ends with a reflection on fear—fear of trust, intimacy, and love. The protagonist acknowledges this fear as a barrier to true healing and fulfillment, leaving a sense of unresolved tension.

---

## Therapeutic Techniques and Insights:

### 1. Grounding and Mindfulness:

The protagonist could benefit from grounding techniques to stay present, reducing his reliance on escapism through substances and constant travel.

### 2. Inner Child Work:

Addressing unresolved childhood trauma through therapeutic methods like inner child work could help unpack the roots of his pain and rebuild a more authentic identity.

### 3. Journaling for Reflection:

Regular journaling could help the protagonist explore his feelings, document prophetic insights, and track his growth. This would also provide clarity on his fears and dreams.

### 4. Building Authentic Connections:

Therapy could guide the protagonist toward rebuilding trust by cultivating relationships based on honesty and vulnerability, rather than maintaining a facade.

### 5. Cognitive Behavioral Therapy (CBT):

CBT techniques could challenge the protagonist's self-limiting beliefs, such as imposter syndrome, and replace them with affirming thoughts that align with his talents and achievements.

---

**Closing Reflection:**

The chapter is a raw and candid exploration of the protagonist's internal struggles and external pursuits. It encapsulates the tension between running from pain and running toward purpose. Through a blend of psychological insight, spiritual guidance, and therapeutic strategies, the protagonist is positioned at a crossroads, ready to confront the fears and truths that will ultimately lead to healing and self-acceptance.

# Chapter 5

# INSIGHT - FAVOR IN MY LOWEST

**Summary:**

This chapter centers around the theme of divine favor amidst adversity. It recounts how the author, despite being at a low point emotionally, mentally, and spiritually, receives an extraordinary opportunity to perform as an opening act for reggae dancehall superstar Sean Paul. This moment symbolizes the paradox of favor appearing in life's darkest hours and serves as a testament to faith, resilience, and the power of prayer.

The chapter delves into the author's struggles with identity and addiction, highlighting how vices like drinking and smoking became coping mechanisms to numb the pain of depression and life's challenges. Even while wrestling with internal battles, the author maintains ambition and a sense of purpose rooted in a steadfast belief in God's presence.

The narrative unfolds with the preparation for the show, the nervous anticipation, and the heartfelt prayer that sets the tone for a transformative night. Arriving at the prestigious College Music Hall in New Haven, Connecticut, the author experiences a mix of self-doubt and pride, bolstered by a profound sense of destiny. The performance itself becomes a defining moment, where the author's talent and presence captivate the audience, marking the beginning of recognition from both peers and industry insiders.

After the performance, a chance encounter with Sean Paul's best friend leads to a personal introduction to the reggae icon. In a moment rich with symbolism, Sean Paul dons the author's custom "Langu" glasses, validating the author's artistry and entrepreneurship while affirming their belief in divine orchestration. The night culminates in an invitation to collaborate in the studio, further cementing the feeling of God's grace at work.

The chapter closes with reflections on the unique challenges faced by those with a prophetic calling. A conversation with a producer reveals the deeper spiritual significance of the author's trials, affirming that their music carries a powerful message meant to impact lives. This revelation underscores the chapter's central message: even in the midst of struggle, there is purpose and divine favor at play.

---

**Themes:**

1. **Divine Favor in Adversity:**

   o The chapter emphasizes that God's grace can manifest even during life's lowest moments, offering opportunities that defy human understanding.

   o The narrative highlights how faith and prayer can unlock blessings, even when external circumstances seem bleak.

2. **Identity and Self-Worth:**

   o The author grapples with self-doubt and questions the worthiness of success. This struggle mirrors a universal journey of reconciling personal value with external validation.

   o The dichotomy between public perception and private struggles is explored, shedding light on the masks people wear to navigate their pain.

3. **Faith as a Source of Strength:**

   o The story illustrates the importance of leaning on faith as a foundation for resilience and perseverance.

   o Moments of prayer and spiritual encounters affirm the author's belief in a higher purpose guiding their journey.

4. **Humility and Service:**

   o The chapter underscores the importance of remaining humble, even when favor elevates one to new heights.

   o The author's willingness to cheer for others and stay grounded reflects the values of humility and community.

---

**Psychological Insights:**

1. **The Role of Vision in Overcoming Adversity:**

   o The author's ability to visualize success during prayer serves as a powerful psychological tool, reinforcing confidence and reducing anxiety before the performance.

2. **The Mask of Functionality:**

   o The chapter explores the phenomenon of high-functioning individuals who maintain ambition and productivity despite battling internal struggles, a common feature of depression and anxiety.

3. **Cognitive Reframing:**

   o The author reframes challenges as part of a divine plan, which provides hope and a sense of purpose amidst the difficulties.

4. **The Psychological Weight of Favor:**

   o Being seen as a "star" by others creates both pressure and isolation, as the author navigates the tension between public admiration and private vulnerabilities.

---

## Therapeutic Techniques Highlighted:

### 1. Mindfulness and Gratitude:

   o The author takes moments to pause and reflect on their blessings, reinforcing gratitude as a coping mechanism for stress and self-doubt.

### 2. Faith-Based Affirmations:

   o Repeating faith-driven affirmations ("God is with me," "This is destiny") helps maintain focus and confidence.

### 3. Spiritual Visualization:

   o The prayerful visualization of success before the performance serves as a therapeutic exercise, reducing fear and reinforcing faith in a positive outcome.

### 4. Storytelling as Healing:

   o Sharing personal struggles and victories with others, both in the dressing room and the studio, fosters connection and reinforces resilience through vulnerability.

---

## Key Quotes and Reflections:

- **"When it's your moment to shine, expect the devil to show up."**

   o This reflects the idea that challenges often intensify just before a breakthrough, encouraging perseverance.

- **"Cheer for others, don't become so consumed in ego and pride that you stop being humble."**
  - o A reminder of the importance of humility and community, even in moments of personal triumph.
- **"God uses you, and he can use others around you, sometimes we don't recognize it."**
  - o This underscores the interconnectedness of life and the ways in which divine guidance can appear through unexpected sources.

---

This chapter serves as a testament to the power of faith, resilience, and the belief that purpose can be found even in the most challenging circumstances. It's a powerful reminder that favor is not about perfection, but about persistence and alignment with a higher calling.

# Chapter 6

# INSIGHT - JUST IN TIME

**Chapter 6 Summary: "Hindsight – Just in Time"**

This chapter explores the profound turning point in the author's life, highlighting the interplay between despair, divine intervention, and personal transformation. While grappling with external success and internal turmoil, the author reflects on how faith and surrender to God rescued him "just in time."

**Themes**

1. **Duality of Success and Struggle:** Despite the perception of success following his performance with Sean Paul, the author reveals a stark contrast between outward achievements and inner despair, emphasizing how external accolades cannot heal internal wounds.

2. **Divine Intervention and Spiritual Awakening:** The author experiences a powerful spiritual encounter, seeing visions of God's protection throughout his life, which catalyzes his repentance and reconnection with his faith.

3. **Temptation and Spiritual Resilience:** Offers of fame and fortune challenge the author's commitment to his beliefs, echoing biblical narratives of temptation and reinforcing the importance of staying true to one's faith.

4. **Transformation Through Service:** By redirecting his focus toward helping others and embracing his role within the church, the author discovers healing and purpose, signifying the redemptive power of community and service.

---

## Psychological Insights

1. **Cognitive Dissonance:** The author's experience of public success versus personal turmoil illustrates the conflict between perceived and internal realities. This disparity often exacerbates feelings of depression and isolation.

2. **Catalyst Moments in Recovery:** The vision of God's intervention acts as a "breaking point," initiating the process of self-reflection and change. Such moments are common in recovery narratives, where an epiphany or spiritual experience provides clarity.

3. **Trauma and Healing Through Confession:** By confessing his struggles with addiction and seeking forgiveness from others, the author begins to release guilt and rebuild his sense of self-worth.

4. **Power of Role Reclamation:** Returning to preaching, a role from his childhood, symbolizes a return to authenticity and purpose, reinforcing his identity as a person of faith.

---

## Therapeutic Techniques Reflected

1. **Journaling and Reflection:** The author's reflections on past decisions, paired with writing music and revisiting scripture, serve as tools for processing trauma and rediscovering hope.

2. **Spirituality in Recovery:** The chapter emphasizes how faith can serve as a protective factor against addiction, offering both accountability and comfort.

3. **Social Support Systems:** Reconnecting with the church community and engaging in service provides structure and emotional support critical for sustained recovery.

4. **Acceptance and Commitment Therapy (ACT):** The author exemplifies the principles of ACT by accepting his flaws and committing to living a values-driven life aligned with his faith.

---

## Key Turning Points

- **Vision of Divine Intervention:** This supernatural experience highlights the author's realization of God's protection and the urgent need for change.

- **Confronting Temptation:** The rejection of the producer's offer to forsake faith mirrors biblical trials, reinforcing the author's spiritual resolve.

- **Joining the Church Community:** The author's decision to serve the church marks the beginning of his transformation, providing a sense of belonging and purpose.

- **Preaching and Healing:** Overcoming his self-perceived unworthiness, the author steps into a leadership role in the church, symbolizing his spiritual growth and newfound confidence.

---

## Notable Quotes and Lessons

1. *"Hurt people hurt people"* – A profound acknowledgment of the cyclical nature of pain and the need for healing.

2. *"It doesn't matter how long it takes or if I never get there, I will never not profess my love and belief in Jesus Christ of Nazareth."* – A declaration of unwavering faith, embodying the power of spiritual resilience.

3. *"God showed up for me just in time."* – A reminder that hope and redemption can emerge even in life's darkest moments.

---

This chapter serves as a powerful testament to how faith and self-accountability can transform despair into hope. It provides a narrative of redemption that resonates with anyone seeking to overcome their struggles, find purpose, and reclaim their life.

# Chapter 7

# INSIGHT - THE DREAM LINE

**Chapter 7 Summary: "Hindsight – The Dream Line"**

This chapter delves into the journey of a dreamer, emphasizing faith, perseverance, and the transformative power of trusting God. It reflects on the challenges and lessons encountered along the path of realizing one's divine calling and underscores how these experiences shape character and purpose.

---

**Themes**

1. **The Dreamer's Journey:** The chapter frames life as a "dream line," where each step, especially the challenges, contributes to personal and spiritual growth.

2. **Faith and Surrender:** It highlights the importance of surrendering control to God and trusting His plan, even in moments of uncertainty.

3. **Resilience Through Grace:** The narrative emphasizes finding strength in weakness through God's grace, illustrating how trials refine faith.

4. **The Role of Forgiveness:** Letting go of past hurts and extending grace to others is shown as essential for healing and fulfilling one's purpose.

5. **Alignment With God's Purpose:** The chapter stresses that success and elevation come from aligning with God's will and nurturing a relationship with Him.

---

## Psychological Insights

1. **Resilience Through Adversity:** The author describes how seasons of struggle build emotional and spiritual resilience, a key factor in personal growth.

2. **Cognitive Reframing:** By viewing challenges as opportunities for growth and preparation, the author shifts his perspective from despair to hope.

3. **Identity and Purpose:** The journey involves questioning one's identity and finding clarity through understanding one's creation in God's image.

4. **Transformational Leadership:** The realization that trials are part of a divine plan enables the author to lead and inspire others with authenticity and compassion.

---

## Therapeutic Techniques Reflected

1. **Mindfulness and Self-Reflection:** Through introspection and prayer, the author identifies patterns in his life and aligns them with God's plan.

2. **Radical Acceptance:** Accepting that struggles are part of the journey facilitates healing and fosters a deeper reliance on faith.

3. **Building a Support Network:** The role of community and prophetic words emphasizes the importance of encouragement and validation from others.

4. **Journaling as Processing:** Writing this book is itself an act of reflection and healing, a method of sharing lessons and insights with others.

---

## Key Turning Points

1. **Surrendering Control:** The author reaches a breaking point, realizing that his own understanding and efforts are insufficient without God's guidance.

2. **Forgiveness and Healing:** A pivotal moment comes as he actively seeks forgiveness and releases resentment, even extending grace to himself.

3. **Alignment With God's Vision:** The author transitions from personal ambitions to fulfilling God's plan, finding purpose in ministry and service.

4. **Faith Amidst Challenges:** Trusting God despite adverse circumstances marks a significant milestone in the author's spiritual growth.

---

## Notable Quotes and Lessons

1. *"When you realize that nothing just happens and God has a plan for your life, you begin to find strength in weak moments."* – A reminder of God's sovereignty and the redemptive nature of struggles.

2. *"The journey isn't told to the dreamer or the visionary. The journey is based on your actions. The journey is based on your faith."* – Faith is the cornerstone of the dreamer's path.

3. *"If it had not been for the Lord God on my side, where would I be?"* – A testimony of God's sustaining grace throughout life's difficulties.

4. *"If you want to go higher in life, go deeper in Christ."* – A call to prioritize spiritual depth for personal and professional elevation.

---

## Practical Takeaways for Dreamers

1. **Faith Over Sight:** Trust in God's promises, even when circumstances appear bleak or uncertain.

2. **The Power of Introspection:** Regularly reflect on your heart and motives to ensure alignment with God's will.

3. **Extend Grace Freely:** Forgiveness is essential for personal freedom and effective ministry.

4. **Nurture Your Relationship With God:** Deep prayer, fasting, and studying scripture are foundational for clarity and strength.

5. **Embrace Challenges as Preparation:** View difficulties as steps toward the fulfillment of your purpose.

---

This chapter serves as an inspiring guide for dreamers and visionaries, encouraging perseverance and faith in the face of adversity. It affirms that challenges are not roadblocks, but building blocks for achieving God's higher purpose. Through reflection, surrender, and dedication to God's word, the author offers a path for others to follow, demonstrating that dreams aligned with faith can lead to transformative impact.

# CLOSING

## DOWN IS UP THE

## EXPERIENCE

### Closing Remarks: Welcome to Down Is Up – The Experience

I hope that as you journeyed through this book, you found something meaningful—something that speaks to you. Dreams are powerful, and everyone should have one. Throughout these pages, I've shared insights and moments that I believe can serve as pearls of wisdom, guiding you through life's own twists and turns.

But this book is just the beginning.

Down Is Up: The Experience is an immersive, multi-dimensional journey that extends beyond these pages, weaving together my story, my music, and a powerful visual narrative. Inspired by both the biblical story of Joseph and my personal journey, this experience brings to life the themes of struggle, perseverance, and divine purpose through a unique blend of storytelling and soul-stirring melodies.

At the heart of this experience is the *Down Is Up* EP—an album that echoes the very essence of this book. Each song reflects pivotal moments in my journey, helping listeners connect deeply with the emotions and lessons within these pages. Whether you are simply someone who enjoys music or you are seeking encouragement in your own trials, this one-of-a-kind experience is designed to move both the heart and soul.

Visually, Down Is Up embraces a retro 70s aesthetic, inspired by the 1971 Jesus Revolution—a time of revival, radical faith, and unity. The colors, fashion, and artistic style evoke a sense of nostalgia while reminding us that spiritual awakenings are timeless. But the retro theme isn't just about aesthetics—it symbolizes a return to raw, authentic faith, mirroring how the music and storytelling guide us back to the essence of God's plan.

This is more than a book, more than an EP—it's an encounter. It's a movement, a call to revival for all who read, listen, and watch *Down Is Up*.

Alongside this book and EP, I am also bringing the story to life visually, creating a powerful representation of *Down Is Up* through film and performance. This moment is one of reflection and breakthroughs. Whether through song, story, or sight, *Down Is Up:* The Experience is meant to uplift, inspire, and remind us that sometimes, the only way up... is down.

www.ingramcontent.com/pod-product-compliance
Lightning Source LLC
Chambersburg PA
CBHW051213120626
46547CB00013B/1334